TWAYNE'S WORLD AUTHORS SERIES

A Survey of the World's Literature

Sylvia E. Bowman, Indiana University

GENERAL EDITOR

SPAIN

Gerald Wade, Vanderbilt University

EDITOR

rl-26

gk

Lucas Fernández

(TWAS 251)

TWAYNE'S WORLD AUTHORS SERIES (TWAS)

The purpose of TWAS is to survey the major writers —novelists, dramatists, historians, poets, philosophers, and critics—of the nations of the world. Among the national literatures covered are those of Australia, Canada, China, Eastern Europe, France, Germany, Greece, India, Italy, Japan, Latin America, the Netherlands, New Zealand, Poland, Russia, Scandinavia, Spain, and the African nations, as well as Hebrew, Yiddish, and Latin Classical literatures. This survey is complemented by Twayne's United States Authors Series and English Authors Series.

The intent of each volume in these series is to present a critical-analytical study of the works of the writer; to include biographical and historical material that may be necessary for understanding, appreciation, and critical appraisal of the writer; and to present all material in clear, concise English—but not to vitiate the scholarly content of the work by doing so.

Lucas Fernández

By JOHN LIHANI
University of Kentucky

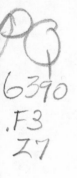

Twayne Publishers, Inc.   ::   New York

To My Three Sons

To My Two Sons

Preface

In his time Lucas Fernández had considerable impact on what might be termed the "vernacularization" of the Renaissance drama in Spain. Until his period the vernacular drama that had existed was limited to the occasionally libertine *juegos de escarnio* (mockery plays) which were somewhat akin to the *commedia dell'arte* so popular in Spain after its importation from Italy, and to the popular mummers who offered a kind of variety show delightful to all types of audiences. The concurrent dramas that flourished in a more serious vein were still being written mostly in Latin and performed, as were the classical dramas of Plautus and Terence, in the halls of universities, schools and cloisters. Also, the liturgical drama of the church coexisted parallel to the theater of a more secular orientation. Both liturgical and secular plays were produced during the period extending from the twelfth through the fifteenth century in Latin and the vernacular languages. Most of those plays have been lost, but with the advent of printing more of them were preserved. The result was an increasing corpus of dramatic literature, especially of the vernacular type. And so we now know of such writers as Iñigo de Mendoza, Juan del Encina, Bartolomé de Torres Naharro, Gil Vicente, and, of course, the central figure of our study, Lucas Fernández.

It was Lucas' good fortune to attend the same university, study with the same mentors, and finally work with many of the same people as did Juan del Encina. Both men served as entertainers and directors of festivities in the palace of the second Duke of Alba during the closing decade of the fifteenth century. Lucas was received with greater favor than Juan when he tried his hand in their native region as the director of public entertainments and even as cantor of the Salamancan cathedral. Due to personal disappointments his rival then left the city to seek a better fortune elsewhere. Encina first tried his luck in Portugal and eventually made his way to Italy. As a result, Fernández' influence grew among the Spanish and Portuguese dramatists, and although Encina's contributions to drama, poetry, and music were large, his traditional title of "the patriarch of the Spanish theater" should be shared with others of his contemporaries.

Lucas Fernández' contributions concerned not only the expansion and elaboration of the theatrical devices already in use, but also the invention of others. Scholars of our time recognize the foundation he helped to establish for the later vernacular theater as this evolved in the gifted hands of the great Golden Age dramatists, such as Lope de Vega, Tirso de Molina, and their followers.

The University of Kentucky   J. LIHANI

Acknowledgments

Like a man, no book is an island unto itself. The acknowledgments for this study are numerous. They start with the renowned Hispanist, the late Professor M. Romera-Navarro, devoted scholar and warm friend, who sparked my interest in the Spanish Renaissance theater—and they extend to the present Spanish editor of the TWAS series, Professor Gerald E. Wade, for his assiduous contributions and patient attention to this book. The complete acknowledgments include my many mentors, colleagues and students, who in one way or another have contributed to this study. Further, the recognition extends to the universities of Texas, Yale, Pittsburgh, and Kentucky that have made awards and research grants which directly or indirectly aided in the elaboration of this work. Finally, I am indebted to my esteemed friend and colleague, Professor John E. Keller, who found in his very busy schedule time to read the entire manuscript of this work and to make most helpful comments and suggestions on it.

Contents

Contents

Chronology

1474 Lucas Fernández is born, probably in the month of October, in the city of Salamanca. Isabella is crowned Queen of Spain in Segovia.

1484– Juan del Encina is choirboy in the Cathedral of Salamanca,

1485 and about this time Lucas probably joins the choral group.

1489 Lucas is orphaned and his uncle Alfonso González de Cantalapiedra, takes charge of his education.

1490 Encina becomes choral director.

1492 Wars of Spanish reconquest come to an end with the fall of Moorish Granada to the Catholic Kings. Columbus discovers the New World. Lucas probably attends the University of Salamanca and works as part-time actor with Juan del Encina.

1495 About this time Lucas obtains the Bachelor's degree from the University of Salamanca.

1496 Lucas, in the palace of the second Duke of Alba, Don Fadrique Álvarez de Toledo, writes his first play, *Comedia (Comedy)*. Probably begins work on a song-drama and several other plays. Juana, second daughter of the Catholic Kings, marries Philip, Archduke of Flanders.

1497 Lucas presents the song-drama, *Diálogo para cantar (Dialogue for Singing)*, and his second play, *Farsa o cuasi comedia (Farce or Quasi Comedy)* of the Doncella, Pastor and the Caballero (known also as the *Farsa de la Doncella* [*The Maiden's Farce*] or the *Farsa del Caballero* [*Farce of the Gentleman*]). On March 19, Prince Juan, son of the Catholic Kings, marries Princess Margaret of Austria in Burgos.

1498 Lucas Fernández obtains the job of cantor, shared with two other youths, at the Cathedral of Salamanca in competition with Juan del Encina. Isabel, eldest daughter of the Catholic Kings, marries Manuel I of Portugal. Encina probably goes to Portugal before heading for Italy.

1499   The terminal year for Lucas to introduce his third play, at Christmas, *Farsa o cuasi comedia (Farce or Quasi Comedy)* of Prabos, Antona and the Soldado (known both as *Farsa de Prabos* [*Farce of Prabos*] and the *Farsa del Soldado* [*Farce of the Soldier*]; we refer to it as the *Farce of Prabos and the Soldier*).

1500   Lucas' *Égloga o farsa del nacimiento de Nuestro Redentor Jesucristo (Eclogue or Farce of the Nativity of Our Redeemer, Jesus Christ)*, referred to in our study as *Égloga del nacimiento (Eclogue of the Nativity)*, is performed, probably in the Cathedral of Salamanca, for Christmas. In October, Lucas probably attends the wedding of Princess María, who marries her former brother-in-law, Manuel I, in Portugal.

1501   In May, the Bishop of Salamanca with other dignitaries accompanies the fourth daughter of the Catholic Sovereigns, Catherine of Aragón, to London for her marriage to the Prince of Wales. Possibly in honor of this marriage Lucas' *Comedy* is presented as part of the entertainment on Corpus Christi day in Salamanca. Lucas is named full cantor and gets an increase in salary. At Christmas time he probably presents his *Auto o farsa del nacimiento de Nuestro Señor Jesucristo (Play or Farce of the Nativity of Our Lord Jesus Christ*, referred to in our study as *Auto del nacimiento (Play of the Nativity)*.

1502   Lucas' guardian-uncle dies and leaves him the benefice of Alaraz plus diverse properties. Encina contests the positions of cantor and organist in the Salamancan Cathedral. Lucas may be entering the clerical profession. He probably goes to Lisbon and participates in Gil Vicente's production of the *Auto pastoril castellano*.

1503   A play presented by Lucas Fernández on Corpus Christi day is probably the *Farce of Prabos and the Soldier*. This would be the terminal year for the composition of the *Auto de la Pasión (The Passion Play)*.

1504   Queen Isabella dies.

1507   Lucas Fernández is described for the first time as a cleric.

He no longer is cantor in the Cathedral. One of his brothers dies.

1511 Henry VIII of England sends fifteen hundred soldiers to his father-in-law, Ferdinand the Catholic, for a war in Africa.

1512 Lucas' residence in Salamanca is documented in a permit to remodel his house.

1513 The parish of Alaraz sues Lucas to reestablish two chaplaincies for the church. Encina returns to Málaga from Rome.

1514 Fernández publishes a compilation of his plays, *Farsas y églogas al modo y estilo pastoril y castellano (Farces and Eclogues in the Pastoral and Castilian Style);* in the textual quotes we cite our recent edition of this work simply as *Farsas;* the fascimile edition we cite as *Farsas,* ed. Cotarelo. By 1514 Lucas acquires the important benefice of Sto. Tomás Cantuariense in Salamanca and is given an additional benefice of San Antolín just outside the city walls.

1515 Lucas receives a letter of privileges from King Manuel of Portugal to establish hotels in Regoim where he has established residence.

1516 Lucas figures in the last will and testament of Queen María of Portugal. Ferdinand the Catholic dies; Charles I is crowned King of Spain.

1517 Martin Luther rebels against Papal authority.

1519 Juan del Encina is ordained priest and celebrates his first Mass in Jerusalem.

1520 Lucas Fernández is named abbot of the clergy of Salamanca and becomes a member of its governing Council.

1522 Takes over post as professor of music at the University of Salamanca left vacant by the death of Diego de Fermoselle, brother of Juan del Encina. Henceforward till his death he becomes closely involved with the varied affairs of the University.

1523 Receives extra compensation for his share in a Thanksgiving service at the University to commemorate the Spanish victory over the French at Fuenterrabía.

1524 He is again mentioned in a document as beneficiary of Alaraz. His second brother dies and is buried in the cloister of the Cathedral of Salamanca.

1526   Lucas is granted a Master's degree in music. This qualifies him to receive the full salary of the chair in music at the University.

1530   Encina dies in León where he served as prior of the Cathedral.

1533   Fernández is in charge of the University festivities on May 6. Probably organizes entire program and personally takes charge of its musical portions.

1542   Lucas Fernández dies on September 17 and is buried in the old Cathedral of Salamanca.

CHAPTER 1

Lucas Fernández: His Life and Times
(1474-1542)

I   The Restless Years

WHEN Lucas Fernández was born, probably in the year
1474, printing by means of movable type had already been
used for almost a generation. The new invention had helped
awaken Europe to a sense of great adventure; the continent was
making triumphant new gestures in the elevation of learning and
of culture to a level heretofore unknown. It was a period of gi-
gantic, indeed, colossal events, with discoveries, explorations, and
conquests not only in the New World, but all over the globe.
There came about thrilling changes in the political and social life
as well as in the economic condition of the various countries of
the continent. This was particularly true in Spain, where Isabella
the Catholic was crowned Queen of Castile in the very year that
Lucas was born. Likewise in that same year, the first book to be
published in Spain came out in Valencia. Lucas Fernández lived
in an epoch of revolutionary changes that touched upon the major
activities of life.

The general store of recorded knowledge pertaining to the
culture and the history of the concluding years of the fifteenth
century and the initial years of the sixteenth is considerable, but
we know relatively little about the life of Lucas Fernández. What
little we do know is due almost entirely to the magnificent biographical essay done by the eminent professor emeritus and former administrator of the University of Salamanca, Dr. Ricardo
Espinosa Maeso.[1] Don Ricardo spent long, tedious, but, at the
same time, patient and rewarding hours in reading and studying
the daily expense records and the minutes of the Church Council
meetings in the archives of the Cathedral of Salamanca. The
archives, now housed in the library of the University of that city,
fill many volumes; they are recorded in the typical script of the

late fifteenth and early sixteenth centuries, and are still clearly legible to one accustomed to the peculiarities of the hand in which they are written. From the expense records and Council minutes, Don Ricardo was able to sift out items relevant to Lucas Fernández. His was truly a labor of love of his youthful days, and it has illuminated for us very aptly not only the life of our poet and dramatist, but also the customs of the period in Salamanca. Don Ricardo's is the only documented, reliable source which we possess of the still largely unknown life of the dramatist, whom Manuel Cañete called the "Calderón" of the early Spanish theater.[2]

The exact day and place of birth of Lucas Fernández are still shrouded in some mystery, but from documentary evidence it seems that, as stated above, he was born in the year 1474 in the architecturally medieval city of Salamanca, widely known since the thirteenth century for its famous university. The year in question is substantiated by the fact that in 1534 Fernández declared in a legal affidavit made in Valladolid that he was then sixty years old.[3] We may infer from his Christian name that he may very well have been born on the saint's day whose name he was to bear. This was a traditional practice for choosing the name for a child. Thus we could possibly surmise that the date of his birth was St. Luke's day, October 18. If he was christened two weeks after birth, as is the custom, and named on that day after the saint, then one could propose an alternate date for his birth as the fourth of the month. Salamanca is regarded with some assurance as the place of his birth since, in the plays that he published there in 1514, he announced on the title page that they were written by "Lucas Fernández, salmantino."[4]

As for the mother of Lucas Fernández, María Sánchez, we know only that she was the wife of Alonso González[5] and that in 1486 she and her husband received from the estate of her brother, Juan Martínez de Cantalapiedra, a life income from some houses. But María Sánchez died in 1489 and the houses came under the trusteeship of the Cathedral Council. María had three brothers, all of whom were men with ecclesiastical positions in Salamanca. One of them was also a professor of music at the University.

We have only sparse information on Lucas Fernández' father, Alonso González,[6] but it is known that in addition to being a carpenter he was also a woodcarver. According to the church records for 1472, he had been living in and renting houses from the Church Council of the Cathedral of Salamanca. He surrendered these to the Council in the same year, and leased others apparently less expensive. But when in 1486 he and his wife received the windfall from their late brother, Juan Martínez, he reclaimed the first ones. In November of 1489, Alonso González followed his wife to the grave. Both probably were victims of the dreaded pestilence that had begun to assail Salamanca in September of that year and continued to ravage it for some time thereafter.

Following a fairly common practice in Spain during the latter part of the fifteenth century, Lucas Fernández changed his paternal name, González, and the maternal Sánchez de Cantalapiedra, to the one under which he was to become known through his writings. For many preceding generations, the first, or baptismal name, was usually the one by which a man was known in his home town. It was considered sufficient to identify him clearly. In many of the papers of the Cathedral of Salamanca our author is referred to merely as "Lucas," or "Lucas el cantor."

Lucas' adoption of the name Fernández seems to have been not entirely arbitrary; there is a trace of the name in the family genealogy. One of Lucas' brothers is at one time referred to in a ledger as Martín González and at another place in the same book as Martín Fernández.[7] This brother, probably younger than Lucas (another, also younger, died by drowning in 1507 or 1508), was a choirboy and later choir chaplain in the Cathedral of Salamanca. One of his duties was that of servicing the organs, which shows that he too might have been a musician like Lucas. This brother died in August of 1524.

There is another possible way of explaining the changes in name that took place then. Many Spaniards at the time were converted either from Judaism or from Islam to Christianity in order to escape the persecution that was heaped upon them by the representatives of the police and of the Inquisition, as well as by the populace itself. Although religious conversion was not a guarantee against continued persecution, or even from ultimate expulsion from the country at the hands of a sometimes whimsical administration, many converts were nevertheless permitted to occupy important positions and to rise to heights of power.

Often, the new convert would take for his own new name the name of his sponsor at the christening. This, however, was probably not the reason for the change in name for Lucas. There is no sound reason for assuming that he was a convert; on only one occasion is there an individual of another faith mentioned in connection with Lucas Fernández. This is to be read in an affidavit in which a *morisca* (Moorish woman) is supplied as a witness.[8] Professor Américo Castro has suggested that Lucas Fernández was a *converso* (converted Jew) who was fortunate in achieving success in his career. He bases this belief on the author's use of the phrase, *los campos tienen ojos,/ llenguas y orejas rastrojos* [9] (the fields have eyes, the stubbles, tongues and ears), which Castro claims was a phrase peculiarly applicable to Jews who had constant fear of persecution. Few would be convinced by such meager testimony.[10]

In any event, the worth of Lucas Fernández' literary work is not directly dependent on whether or not he was a *converso*. Indeed, the chances of his being one would seem to be denied by certain documents published by Ricardo Espinosa. These documents show that all his uncles were ecclesiastics in Salamanca. One uncle was a professor of music (Martín González de Cantalapiedra), the other two (Juan Martínez de Cantalapiedra and Alonso González de Cantalapiedra) were canons and alternately chaplains, priests, and majordomos. All were obviously staunch Christians who occupied high positions of trust in the parish of the church of Salamanca.[11] Furthermore, Juan Martínez as a canon in 1472 received a favorable judgment against a citizen of Cantalapiedra to collect the fruits of a certain benefice. The citizen is designated as "Abraham de Palencia, Jew." [12] In no document referring to the family or relatives of Lucas Fernández do we find a similar designation. The relationship between the *morisca* of reference above and Lucas' family remains to be established. Thus, it seems reasonable to assert that since the identity of a person as a Jew was made a point of importance in one document, the same type of identification would be expected in other documents involving Lucas Fernández, if a Jew was concerned in the matter. It has not been established, therefore, that he was partly of Jewish (or Morisco) blood.

It was in 1489, then, that Lucas and his brothers became orphans when both parents died. The sole surviving uncle of the

three on the mother's side,[13] Alonso González de Cantalapiedra,
took charge of the orphaned boys and looked after them until his
own death in 1502. It was probably in 1490 that Lucas started
out as a choirboy in the Cathedral of Santa María and pursued
the course of liberal arts toward the Bachelor's degree at the
University of Salamanca. The degree in due time qualified him
for the priesthood.[14] His singing teacher was probably Fernando
de Torrijos, who held the office of cantor in the cathedral and
whose duties included the teaching of singing to the choirboys.
His music teacher at the University was probably the brother of
Juan del Encina, Diego de Fermoselle, who held the post of
professor of music until August, 1522.[15]

The records show that by 1484 Lucas had already taken part
in churchly events of one sort or another, when he, apparently
along with other boys (all of them around the age of ten), com-
mitted some mischief in the church by breaking a scepter and
some censer chains.

Lucas dedicated himself to poetry and music from the time of
his university years, and eventually went on to become the chapel
organist for Queen María, one of the four daughters of the Catholic Kings, and the second wife of the King of Portugal, Don
Manuel I. It was probably Lucas' interest in poetry and music
that drew him also to the ducal palace in the farming town of
Alba de Tormes, and it is quite possible that while there he acted
in the early plays written by Juan del Encina for the pleasure of
the Duke's court.[16] It wasn't long until Lucas himself took up the
pen in emulation of and competition with Encina. His own plays
were presented as early as 1496, when Encina, six years his
senior, was still with the Duke's household as director and master
of ceremonies of its many festivities and public celebrations.

Lucas was twenty-four years old when in 1498 he managed to
secure for himself the position of cantor at the Cathedral, a
position to which Juan del Encina had also aspired. The competition for position of cantor had acquired the proportions of a
scandal. We shall examine this in detail in the chapter on the
relationships between the two men. In brief, a committee was
appointed to resolve the situation. Influential relatives of Lucas
found a place on it and proceeded to appoint Lucas to the job.
Initially, two other youths were to assume equal shares in the
responsibility, as also in the salary. By 1501, after three years,

Lucas had done so well that the Council decided to double his salary until a permanent cantor could be decided upon. We are not told what happened to the other cantors, but apparently they abandoned their respective shares in the position. Lucas became increasingly active as cantor, even though not on a full-time basis, and gradually added to his participation in the regular festivities of the church, including, as we shall see in a later chapter, those of the Corpus Christi holidays.

Yet all was not sun and roses with Lucas despite the backing of the Council, for in 1502 a certain Francisco de Encina, armed with the power granted him by a Papal Bull in behalf of his brother, Juan del Encina, petitioned the Council, requesting that the place occupied by Lucas as cantor and also that occupied by the church organist, be immediately awarded to Juan del Encina.[17] The Council, however, rather than give in to the demands, decided to appeal the bull, and later even offered to bear the cost of defending its two employees in a suit that was argued before the court of Rome. The outcome of this suit appears to have been uncertain, but Lucas, through the support of the Council, may have remained in the position of cantor at least for a while. In 1507, however, a letter which speaks of the appointment of his brother, Martín González de Cantalapiedra, as chaplain of the choir, also mentions Lucas in the past tense, stating that he had been the cantor of the church. In the meantime, upon the death in 1502 of his benevolent uncle, Alonso González, Lucas inherited additional income in the form of his late uncle's benefice in Alaraz, a town situated east of Salamanca. In 1507 we find him mentioned in the Alaraz Council's records as a cleric, a beneficiary of the curate-benefice in the town.[18] From the archives we know that in 1500 the benefice was worth 1736 *maravedíes* a year, an amount equal to about three months of a soldier's pay. This is not a large sum. The benefice, however, included also the income from four houses which were assigned to the parish. There were also other benefits, such as the use of certain lands. Records for these show that Lucas received rent, paid at first in produce, but later he had it converted into currency when he assigned the lands to the Alaraz Council for their administration.

We know, therefore, that in 1507 Lucas was already an ordained priest, inasmuch as he is referred to as a cleric, and that before 1507 when he was spoken of in the past tense as cantor of the Cathedral of Salamanca, he was probably fulfilling his obligations in Alaraz. There is no evidence to show that Lucas did or did not reside in Alaraz. The village church that in our time serves the community of Alaraz was under construction in 1563; it was completed in 1590. There is no way of knowing when the construction of the church began, but one can well suppose that it may have been at the beginning of the sixteenth century. There is no document today in the church's records that bears the hand of Lucas. The oldest surviving book in the archive is that recording baptisms. The book, badly preserved, lacks the first leaves, so that the earliest legible entries deal with the year 1516.[19] By that time Lucas' benefice in Alaraz had been relinquished and he had embarked on other paths of endeavor for a livelihood, as we shall presently see. It would appear that the arrangement in Alaraz was at best of a temporary or of a part-time nature, and that Lucas resumed or had retained his duties of cantor in Salamanca. This interpretation is supported by an affidavit dated in Salamanca on January 19, 1512, in which he is spoken of as "Lucas, cantor." The document further implies that our author was living at least part of the time in Salamanca, for according to the record, he sought and was given permission to enlarge the space outside his house so that he could get more daylight into it.[20]

Although his residence in Alaraz for any extended length of time is doubtful, his visits to the village are to be assumed. He probably officiated at the mass for certain periods of the year and on some occasions no doubt had emergency calls to the Alaraz parish to hold funerals or christenings, to perform marriages and the like. We see no reason to assume, as some scholars have done, that Lucas never left Salamanca.

It will be remembered that Lucas had been cantor of the church of Salamanca since 1498 and that his uncle died in 1502 leaving him the benefice in Alaraz. So from 1502 he was sustained by two positions. If he found it impossible to comply with the demands of both his jobs as cantor in Salamanca and as curate in Alaraz, he could arrange for a substitute to officiate for him in case of conflict. Lucas did not seem to take his duities in Alaraz with the seriousness that the church's Council desired. Perhaps because he had not established permanent residence there, the local congregation demanded that he put two chaplains in his stead to attend to the augmented business of the parish. He declined to fulfill their demands and the matter was taken to court.

Hence in 1513, almost a dozen years after he obtained the benefice in Alaraz, the local Church Council hired a lawyer to represent its case against Lucas and to insist that he pay greater heed to his obligations in the parish. Lucas hired an attorney, Salvador González, possibly a relative on his father's side, to represent his interests in Alaraz. The hearing before the representative of the bishopric of Salamanca resulted in a verdict demanding that Lucas appoint two chaplains to serve the requirements of his office. The compensation of the benefice was made substantial enough to pay for the services of both,[21] and it was stated that if Lucas should choose to retain one chaplaincy, he could do so and was to appoint one other person so that there would be two ministers to comply with the court's judgment.[22] Through the new arrangement, the Council hoped that the parishioners would be assured of the services of a priest at all times.

The litigation just explained leads us to believe that between 1502 and 1513 Lucas had performed his duties in a more or less satisfactory manner. But by 1513 he was found lacking, and the difficulty that arose was in part due to the fact that Alaraz experienced a small population explosion,[23] a phenomenon for which no explanation is provided. We may suppose that there possibly were several causes: (a) perhaps an influx of strangers to the town, those displaced elsewhere by political or other events, (b) possibly an increased birthrate, (c) perhaps a decrease in the mortality rate, or a combination of all three. In any event, the court stated that if the population were to decrease again, the town would return to one cleric, and the compensation would be reduced accordingly.

Both the attorney for Lucas Fernández and the representative for Alaraz accepted the verdict. This meant in effect that Lucas could continue with his benefice if he wanted to, and indeed in 1524 we still find him mentioned as a *beneficiado* of Alaraz.[24] The only requirement imposed upon him was to provide for two chaplains in continuous service there instead of one. He was given additional compensation, as we have seen, to cover the services of the second cleric. He probably elected at this time to appoint two men in his stead, for he now began to devote much of his time to a new benefice which was granted him in Salamanca by the parish of Santo Tomás Cantuariense in 1514.

We are dealing with this affair in Alaraz at some length to stress Lucas' personal presence there on many and repeated occasions. He did not lead as sheltered a life as some critics have supposed, and he did leave his native city on occasion, not only to go to places within the province of Salamanca, but as we shall see later, also into Portugal.

In 1513 Lucas made a contract to transfer the administration of much of his own benefice into the hands of the Alaraz Council. The document for this transfer shows that Lucas had a personal acquaintance with people from the town, for several came to witness the document. Its contents further reveal his humane concern for the individual welfare of the common townsfolk. The social consciousness of his time is made manifest by the wording of the arrangement for the disposal of the lands under his benefice. It was specified by the parties to the contract that these lands were to be used only by "simple and sanctioned" people (Espinosa, p. 594), and the lands were never to fall to any privileged or powerful individual, and certainly not to a church or school or monastery. Although it is not made clear as to who or how the simple and sanctioned people were to be determined, it was Lucas' desire that the plain folks should be protected and not deprived of the use of the land by the wealthy and the powerful.[25] Lucas felt the same way as did other writers of the day, notable among whom was Bartolomé de Torres Naharro, who may have been a colleague of personal acquaintance to Lucas.

As we have noted, about the year 1514 Lucas Fernández obtained his second benefice, an important one, from the parish of Santo Tomás Cantuariense (St. Thomas of Canterbury) in Salamanca. This was for him a much more conveniently located office than the one in Alaraz, for it was within an easy walking distance from the Cathedral where Lucas' other duties lay. The church of Santo Tomás Cantuariense still stands in the old part of town. On the outside, though the stone steps and terrace together with the balustrade surrounding it are time- and weather-worn, the exterior of the building itself appears to be in excellent condition. Inside, the situation is quite different. The sacristy roof caved in years ago, and although it is being slowly restored, the church, a storage place for the tools and paraphernalia of carpenters and bricklayers, looks more like an abandoned warehouse than like an unused church.

Perhaps because he sensed the demand for more spiritual guidance from his church groups—a demand he had experienced in Alaraz—and also anticipating new commitments in other areas as far away as Portugal, commitments which would tend to interfere with his duties in Salamanca, Lucas undertook to safeguard his faithful flock. In May of 1514 he himself called a meeting of his new parishioners to discuss the establishment of a second chaplaincy for the church of Santo Tomás. As was their custom, the devout were summoned to the special meeting by the ringing of the church bell, and there Lucas explained to them that one benefice was insufficient to attend to the needs of the parish. He urged his faithful members to establish another benefice so that the church would be better served. The congregation agreed, and granted him the continuation of his own benefice while setting up an additional one.

The parishioners of Santo Tomás Cantuariense had been easily persuaded by Lucas to employ two clerics to minister to them, for they had had previous experience when they were forsaken in time of need. They had been left without a priest during particularly adverse and trying times, when, during a pestilence, they sought to make hasty confessions and sought religious consolation. On such painful days the cleric, it seemed, would either hasten out of the city to escape the plague, or he himself would become a victim of it. In such instances the advisability of having two benefices for a perpetual curacy was made clear to the congregation, if it was to receive proper attentions in time of its necessity and sorrow. The congregation in its new agreement with Lucas desired for all concerned to know that it must have a mass said every day of the week, no matter how the two chaplains worked out their own schedules between themselves.[26]

The second chaplain that came to aid Lucas Fernández in the parish of Santo Tomás was from Ávila. He was a namesake on Lucas' mother's side, Lorenzo Sánchez, but it is not known whether there was any family connection between the two and hence whether Lucas favored one who was really a member of his family. A trusted relative in the position would of course prove invaluable while he would be absent possibly attending to business in Portugal.

We are told that Lucas' own benefice in Salamanca consisted of a house and an oven. This structure made of brick was no doubt used by the community for its bread baking, and the users would pay Lucas a fee each time they used it. Lucas' other perquisites included the control of quarries on the River Tormes as well as a vineyard in the vicinity. All of this he possessed and enjoyed during his entire lifetime. According to a document of May 12, 1514, there was also another, though smaller benefice: the parish of San Antolín, located just outside the walls of the city, which paid him a third of the tithes of the church. For this compensation he was expected to conduct twelve masses a year and to lead a special procession from Santo Tomás to San Antolín on the saint's day in whose memory the church was named.

The two benefices in and outside the walls of Salamanca, together with other business endeavors, were a hindrance to Lucas' other cultural and public activities. Yet during the year 1514 he found time to collect his dramas (written between 1496 and 1503) and to have them published on November 10 by an Italian printer of Salamanca, Lorenzo de Liomdedei. Presumably his new book added to Lucas' social prestige, and probably consolidated his position in the parish of Santo Tomás. Although he may have cotinued to write, there are no other surviving texts to testify to later literary productions.

There is evidence that Lucas Fernández was in Portugal, perhaps as early as 1502, although this date has not been documented. In 1500 María, a daughter of the Catholic Kings, had married Manuel I of Portugal, who had earlier been married to her sister, Isabel. With their marriages, there entered many Spaniards into the life of the Portuguese court. Lucas Fernández was probably among those who wended westward with the Spanish political, economic, and cultural interests. His participation in the presentation of the *Auto pastoril castellano (The Castilian Pastoral Play)*, composed by Gil Vicente in Lisbon, is a very likely event. Vicente's play was presented on Christmas of 1502 and reveals strong influence from Lucas Fernández' first comedy. In addition to this hint at Lucas' early presence at the Portuguese court, there is the fact that Queen María named him in her will among her *moços da capella* (chapel youths,) a term probably used to designate anyone employed within the church. In this case it probably included the task of chapel musician. The Queen identified him as a "Castilian" in the book of the members of her household at the time of her death in 1516.[27] Lucas Fernández' presence in the Portuguese court on repeated occasions during Queen María's lifetime is, therefore, indisputable, for the list of employees is given with a stipulated *moradia* (annual lodging rent), suggesting that similar arrangements were made over a period of several years.

It also appears that in 1515 Lucas lived in the town of Regoim in the province of Coimbra in Portugal. The document verifying this fact came to light in our search of the National Archives of the Torre do Tombo, situated in the Palácio da Assembléia Nacional in Lisbon. The volume of the Chancelaria of D. Manuel I contains a copy of a letter, dated the 28th day of May of 1515, sent from the King to a certain Lucas Fernández; in the letter the King gives him certain rights and privileges and permission to enlarge the houses that Lucas possesses with the understanding that he become an *estalajadeiro* (hotel-keeper).[28] Such a letter of privilege falls well within the business pattern that has already been exemplified in Lucas' acute business sense for real estate, houses, and rentals.

After the death of Queen María, Lucas' privileged position in the Portuguese court seems to have become precarious, and his adventurous and active nature led him back once again to Salamanca where in 1520 he was elected abbot of its clergy.

The last third of Lucas Fernández' life is shrouded in mystery, though certainly he did not pass it in obscurity. He was a most active individual as an abbot, priest of Santo Tomás, and part-time priest in San Antolín, a member of the Church Council of Salamanca, and finally, after 1522, a professor of music in the University of Salamanca.

II *Abbacy and University Service*

In his new capacity as abbot, the administrator of a monastery, Lucas Fernández had the right to sit on the Church Council, at that time the most important governing body, religious as well as secular, in Salamanca. In that year (1520) on May first, one of the preoccupations of the Council was a brief which Pope Leo X had granted to the King, Charles I, upon the latter's demand, that he be permitted to bring to trial and to punish members of the clergy by secular law, when this law was transgressed. Lucas Fernández, with the rest of the Church Council, found this innovation unexpected and not to his liking, since he considered it an infringement on ecclesiastical rights. As Fernández and his colleagues saw it, the King was seeking to increase his own power at the expense of the clergy. The Council agreed that a national assembly of all the clergy should be convoked on St. John's day (June 24) in Toledo to act upon the papal decree. The Council likewise agreed that the delegates to the Congress to be sent by their respective churches would have their expenses paid out of Church funds. We are not told the results of the Congress, but presumably it could do nothing to block the absolutist tendencies of the young Charles I.

Records of the University of Salamanca, the secretarial minutes, and others cast occasional light on Lucas' other activities. Thus when on August 9, 1522, Diego de Fermoselle, the brother of Juan del Encina, died and left vacant his post of professor of music at the University, Lucas, after competing for the position with two other candidates, was, on October 31, given the professorship. Since he held only the Bachelor's degree, while his predecessor had the Master's degree, Lucas' salary was determined to be about half that of Fermoselle.

The few records that we have concerning his performance at the University show that Lucas was a conscientious and exemplary teacher. His duties were publicly outlined in the statutes of the University as were those of other professors. Part of the class hour he was to spend teaching or lecturing to the class on the theory of music, and another part in practicing and applying the theory to the music itself. This type of allocation of time was to be in effect from October till March when he was to turn his attention to the teaching of the plain chant.[29] From March till June 24, the concentration on the plain chant was accompanied by studies of organ music, as well as songs accompanied by other types of instrumental music. From then until the close of the school year he was to present the class with studies in counterpoint. In the academic year 1523–24, Lucas was paid an extra sum of money for participating in the Thanksgiving service held at the University in commemoration of the victory the Spanish troops had against the French at Fuenterrabía.

It would appear that Lucas was a man of a strong constitution, and fairly immune to the yearly rounds of illnesses that incapacitate men of lesser physical stamina. He was, moreover, a man of dynamic perseverance, of judicious and cautious exercise of wisdom, a man who loved to be with people and who sought out their company, especially that of young people. As we have seen, he had a keen business sense. He worked hard, knew he was competent, and thus had his fair share of self-esteem. He could be patient under duress. His record of attendance for his University classes offers substantial evidence of his good health and conscientiousness. During nineteen of his twenty years on the faculty, he was absent only twice, but one year, that of 1530–31, brought eleven class absences. We recall that professors were fined for class absences, unless a substitute could be provided, and Lucas seems to have had difficulty in finding a suitable one. There is, however, one record of a substitute; the date was June 28, 1526.[30]

On December 30, 1526, on a Sunday, according to the archives, Lucas was granted his Master's degree in music. He took the oath of a Master before the Archdeacon of Ledesma, the Vice Chancellor of the University, and the doctors and masters who were his colleagues.[31] This event qualified him at the age of fifty-two to receive the full salary of the position of Professor of Music.

From 1525 on, the University found itself to be a hotbed of contention. There arose sharp differences between the Crown and the clergy in Salamanca. The latter were insistent upon governing the University and resented any attempt on the part of representatives of the Crown to encroach upon their powers. We saw earlier that Charles I had successfully gained favor with Pope Leo X, and when the latter died and was succeeded in 1522 by Adrian VI, it seemed that Charles I was destined to continue to have his way since Adrian had served as Charles' tutor. Unfortunately for Charles, Adrian VI lived only a year, and the man who succeeded him on the papal throne, Clement VII, had no love for Charles I. Only after Charles sacked Rome in 1527 and imprisoned the Pope did the latter make peace with him. Trouble erupted when Pope Clement VII appointed a Rector of the University of Salamanca. The local clergy and faculty opposed this particular appointment and, instead, proceeded to elect a Rector of their own preference. The problem of having two Rectors was solved for a brief period when the papal appointee died. However, misunderstandings continued to multiply, and the students, who held a voice in the policies of the University, also entered into the fray. Arrests followed, and the Crown, intent on castigating them for their riotous misbehavior, chose to have their cases heard in the capital of Valladolid. The local faculty and clergy were quick to defend the students, and successfully opposed the King's move.[32]

But the strife continued. The secular government insisted on its own representative in the name of reforms, and Lucas Fernández, this time as earlier, figured among the traditionalists on the faculty bent upon preserving the status quo. He was not ready yet to accept innovations. Lucas participated with the faculty in the election in 1529 for still another new Rector, but the King had sent two observers down to represent him and to see to it that his reforms to strengthen his own hand were carried out. The King's representatives vetoed the election of the Rector but accepted an election of a new Council by the faculty. They then directed the Council to choose a new Rector from an approved list of five names. This the Council did and Charles I had attained the authority over the University that he had sought. It is worthy of notice that when the new statutes of the University were approved, a copy was prepared in calligraphic form and submitted to him.

Lucas, a member of the Faculty Council from 1530 until his death, was present at most of the university-wide faculty meetings. The records show that at one of these meetings Lucas, lamenting the meagerness of funds and the large expenses involved, asked for an increase in the monies allotted to the programs of festivities which were under his direction during the academic year.[33] After study, a committee recommended that the administration provide the necessary funds. Lucas appears to have been an important member of the group that carried forward the University's business.

The records again show that on May 6, 1533, Lucas and a colleague were placed in charge of organizing a procession for the following Sunday. One of the planned attractions was the running of the bulls, similar to the famous modern practice in Pamplona. A professor was put in charge of purchasing the bulls and having them brought to town. There were some faculty members who raised objections to the running of the bulls on the basis of the risks and dangers involved. They maintained that the bulls should have their horns blunted, so that no one would be likely to suffer serious injury. Lucas accepted the exercise only on condition that the bulls also be hobbled, thus further protecting the throngs in the streets. The incident is recalled here as an indication of Lucas' concern for the public welfare, a trait in him that helps to explain the popularity he enjoyed among his colleagues. The sequel to the episode came with the Council's decision to permit only four bulls to run.

Another incident—the year is 1538—serves to throw further light on Lucas' character and attitudes. Charles I instructed the faculty that a certain professor of his choice be given leave of absence to lecture at the University of Coimbra in Portugal; in case of faculty refusal, those responsible would be exiled from the kingdom and their property confiscated.[34] There were twenty-four votes cast on the question of the leave for the professor concerned. Nine members heeded the King's demands, while fifteen votes were cast in favor of entreating him to reconsider his appointment. Lucas' vote was counted among those that acquiesced in the royal wish. By now he had come to recognize the power of the monarchy and to accept the inevitability of the secular government's growing voice in the conduct of the University. His age, sixty-four, probably was a factor in his acquiescence; perhaps he did not care to risk the loss of all that he had worked for so hard. The King, obdurate, persisted in his demands, and the Council had no alternative but to accede. In this fashion Charles destroyed the absolute control of the University by the Church and transferred it to himself.

By 1540–41 Lucas' attendance at the meetings of the faculty Council became less regular. Indeed, during that year he is mentioned but once in the meetings; this is December of 1540. His usually robust health seems to be failing. In the year 1541–42 his name is no longer reported in the sessions of the Council, nor does he come to teach his classes. On September 17 his health has become so frail according to the faculty minutes, that the notes imply the appointment of his successor as Professor of Music. It seems that it was on this same day that Lucas Fernández died: Dr. Espinosa Maeso reveals in his essay that the records of the Church Council for September 18 noted that houses were left vacant as the result of the death of the Master Lucas Fernández.[35] Lucas was sixty-eight years of age. He was buried in the "old" Cathedral of Salamanca. His burial, of the customary kind, was in a grave under the floorstones of the church: Lucas' body would replace the bones of the grave's former occupants; their remains being stacked in one portion of the tomb. In a similar way the playwright's bones were gathered up to make room for a new cadaver, and these remains, mixed with the dust of others who preceded him, have since been scattered and fused with the dust of countless corpses that have followed into the same sepulchre. If at one time the stone slabs that covered the graves beneath the Cathedral's floor bore inscriptions of the names of those who rested below them, those inscriptions have long since been worn off by the feet of those who traversed the nave of the church; there is no trace of Lucas' grave. Nor are there records of burial from the "old" Cathedral to show a plan of the graves and thus make possible the identification of one as the eternal resting place of Lucas Fernández.

CHAPTER 2

Lucas Fernández and Juan del Encina

SOME of the more intriguing aspects of the life of Lucas Fernández are his professional and social contacts with other writers of the day. There is some reason to think that he knew the fine musician, poet, dramatist, and impatient social climber, Juan del Encina (1468–1529). Ricardo Espinosa Maeso has privately suggested that the two were in fact cousins. It is not so certain, but, as we shall see, very likely that Lucas was also acquainted with the goldsmith-poet of the Portuguese court, Gil Vicente (1465–1537?).[1] In this chapter, we shall present some aspects of the personal relationship between Lucas Fernández and Juan del Encina, and of necessity shall repeat certain details from our preceding chapter.

Through the timely intercession of a protector, Juan del Encina was granted employment in the house of the Duke of Alba, first cousin to the Catholic King, Fernando de Aragón. In the ducal court, Encina probably served initially as program director for the entertainment presented on holidays and special occasions: important marriages, christenings, birthdays, anniversaries, and other social events. His official duties gave Encina an opportunity of no little consequence for his future welfare, and he made use of his talents as musician, poet, actor, and impresario. His success was not achieved without certain hindrances; his appointment aroused the envy of other theatrically inclined people who sought the same position during the difficult and trying times when lucrative posts were few and the contenders many. His rivals were further alienated by Encina's ambitious aims and his insatiable desire for ever greater gain and larger rewards commensurate with what he believed to be his capacity. His enemies lost no opportunity to oppose his efforts at poetry and drama, and to indispose him with his employer.[2] Some critics have suggested that one of Encina's enemies may have been Lucas Fernández, his erstwhile friend and companion, and perhaps his cousin, as suggested above. This negative attitude of Fernández toward Encina so early in the former's career has not been established as fact; it may certainly be maintained that, at the least, Fernández' opposition to Encina was hardly an active one at first; it seems to have lacked bitterness or envy, and perhaps was prompted more by a sentimental disappointment in the friend whose personality and attitudes often bred contempt in those who would have preferred to respect him. This dislike of Encina was apparently a generally shared reaction. As indicated by his *Cancionero* of 1496,[3] Encina seems to have been unduly obsequious toward the Duke and Duchess of Alba. Although this attitude was common enough in those times, Encina overdid it. He also promoted his own fortunes too vigorously, and especially before the Duchess, whose vanity he judged to be more susceptible than the Duke's to his praises. It was presumably Encina's unfortunate personality and actions that eventually cost him his position at the ducal palace, and made it difficult for him to achieve other positions in Salamanca.

As for the families of Fernández and Encina, it seems that at first there were rather cordial relations between them. This is suggested by the fact that Fernández' uncle, Martín González de Cantalapiedra, the Salamancan professor of music referred to in our first chapter, named Encina's brother, Diego de Fermoselle, as his substitute when he was unable to meet his classes. This amicable arrangement was, however, terminated apparently because of ill-feeling that arose from professional rivalry. We shall examine in more detail why Fernández and Encina ultimately became enemies.

When, upon the death of their parents, Lucas and his brothers came under the tutelage of their uncle, Alonso, the latter succeeded in providing security for their future by placing the boys in positions where they soon would learn to fend for themselves. The ducal palace afforded Alonso the opportunity. He had connections with the palace primarily because he held the benefice in Alaraz which was under the jurisdiction of the Archpriest of Alba de Tormes. So it was the uncle who opened the palace doors to Lucas. Juan del Encina had by this time worked about three years in the Duke's household; Lucas probably started out as a part-time actor serving on programs directed there by Encina.

When Encina learned of the attempts of the Fernández family to establish Lucas there permanently, he resented them because he felt that his own position was endangered. He made this quite clear in one of his plays (*Égloga* I) from which we present the following colloquial rendition in which Juan speaks for Encina:

MATEO. There you go, putting on airs, now that you've pushed into the palace! You've gone pretty damn far! You think you're good enough for the hall? You don't have it in you.

JUAN. I wasn't born to it! Hush now, mischief-maker; you're always looking for trouble, you and your uncle too.[4]

The falling out between the two families arose directly from the rivalry for the position of cantor of the Cathedral of Salamanca which was left vacant in 1498 by the death of Fernando de Torrijos, the cantor since 1485. Upon Torrijos' death, several candidates appeared; among these were Lucas Fernández and Juan del Encina. The latter speaks to us of the episode in his *Égloga de las grandes lluvias:*

JUAN. And it happened that on that day a sexton died.

RODRIGACHO. Who was the sexton? Tell me.

JUAN. A darn good singer.

ANTÓN. None other.

. . . .

I hope they make you the cantor, now.

RODRIGACHO. The devil will probably give it to you—'cause you got yourself some good masters; every time you come and go, you do pretty good with them.

MIGUELLEJO. They're not good any more except as a pretense; they'll prefer to choose any stranger to you who are from there.

RODRIGACHO. Don't worry, they'll give it to you if they're smart.

. . . .

JUAN. I swear, you just don't understand; there's a lot of people mad at me.

. . . .

Some of them, I don't know why, and others, I don't know how, 'cause I don't hold them any grudge, and I never did.[5]

True enough, the austere atmosphere within the walls of the Church Council's chamber was more helpful to Lucas Fernández' than to Juan del Encina's hopeful dreams. Both men had grown up locally; their virtues and shortcomings were equally well known to the people in the parish. Lucas found himself in a more advantageous position than did Encina, since his uncle, Alonso, was an administrator in the Cathedral and a member of the governing Church Council. In addition, another member of the Council may have been related to Lucas' family. This was Francisco de Salamanca, likewise a church administrator and a person who had great prestige and influence. Both of these ecclesiastics with vested interests in the success of Lucas Fernández would naturally be expected to support his appointment to the position.

Despite this favorable picture for Lucas, it is apparent that his opponent had at least some support in the Council. One of its members, a canon in Salamanca, proposed on the twenty-fourth of October of 1498 that if no one outside of Salamanca were to show interest in the position, Encina should be named cantor of the Cathedral, since, in the canon's opinion, he was the most qualified individual of all the residents of the city.[6] This could have been interpreted as a direct slur against Lucas Fernández, but it had little effect.

The Council resolved the situation by naming a committee of three members to evaluate the competency of the candidates and select a successor from among them. Since Francisco de Salamanca served on the committee, it is surprising that in the end Lucas was not granted the job outright; instead, the committee proposed that the salary of the cantor be divided among three youths, one of whom was Lucas. The minutes of the Council for April 19, 1499, stipulated that the salary should be equally divided into three parts, one for Lucas, one for a youth named Bartolomé, and the third to the son of a blacksmith. The last two who were not identified in any other way, may have been the strangers scoffed at by Encina in the *Égloga*'s passage we translated. These youths were possibly in their late teens or early twenties; Lucas at that time was about twenty-five.

Fernández was content with the decision, but the displeasure that this turn of events brought to Juan del Encina led him to decide on a new course of action. He left Salamanca and the ducal palace at Alba de Tormes in search of more fitting rewards outside of Spain—first in Portugal and later in Italy.

Lucas and the Church Council had not heard nor seen the last of Juan del Encina. Lucas' new position was jeopardized by a suit brought against him by the Encina family. It happened that on the second of December of 1502, while Encina was residing in Rome, he obtained a Papal Bull for his brother, Francisco. Armed with this power, Francisco went before the Salamancan Council and demanded that the Council immediately award Lucas' entire salary and that of an organist, as well, to his brother.[7] If this demand was not satisfactorily met, the Council was informed it would suffer unpleasant consequences. It therefore reluctantly announced its willingness to take up the matter, prudently affirming its willingness to comply with what was proper and just.[8]

The Council's expression of willingness to abide by the bull was less than candid; its members were not disposed to depose either the organist or Lucas Fernández with whose services they were sufficiently pleased to have given him a substantial raise in salary only a year earlier. And so they sided with Fernández despite showing a superficially tolerant attitude to the demands of Juan del Encina. The Council later accused Encina of trying to usurp Lucas' job under false pretenses and with distortion of the facts.[9] A few months later, on February 17, 1503, the Council espoused Lucas' rights to such an extent that it considered the procedure against him a direct affront to the Council itself, and it offered to subsidize his expenses should there be legal action against Lucas. In this way the Council also attempted to assert its right to make its own decisions rather than accept direction from Rome.

It is likely that during the latter portion of the year (1502) Lucas was away in Portugal where he served in various capacities, such as court organist,[10] director of festivities (to celebrate the birth of the new prince, João, later to become João III), and guide of Gil Vicente's budding interest in the art of dramaturgy. He may still have been in Portugal when the Encina family, taking advantage of his absence, made gestures toward taking over his position. He may have remained in Portugal during the Christmas holidays and possibly acted in the Nativity play, *Auto pastoril castellano*, that Gil Vicente prepared at the request of the King's mother, Doña Beatriz.

By February of 1503, Lucas was back in Salamanca. He received notice from the Council that it would back him in his defense of retaining his position as cantor. In view of this support, he decided to contest the Papal Bull. There is evidence that in July of 1503 the case was, in effect, being tried. Lamentably, no record of the decision has been found. It is not known for certain whether it was in Encina's or in Fernández' favor. There is no indication that Encina appeared in Salamanca to undertake the duties of the office that he sought, and yet by 1507 Lucas had for one reason or another at least temporarily vacated the position. A draft of a letter in which Martín González de Cantalapiedra is spoken of as having been named chaplain of the choir contains the explanation that he was "brother of Lucas, cantor, who *was* of this church." [11] So the outcome of the matter remains mysteriously inconclusive. But, as we saw in our Chapter 1, Lucas was by now a cleric, and was also receiving support from an inherited benefice in Alaraz since 1502.

Beyond the items which have been documented by Ricardo Espinosa Maeso,[12] there is only textual and circumstantial information to cast light on Lucas Fernández' life as this impinged on his relationship with Juan del Encina. We have attempted to fill in some of the factual lacunae with a certain amount of reasoned speculation to clarify the connection between these patriarchs of the Spanish theater.

CHAPTER 3

Lucas Fernández and Gil Vicente

I Probable Meetings between the Court Entertainers

THERE is no firmly documented evidence to show Lucas Fernández' acquaintance with Portuguese writers, musicians, and court entertainers, but there are certain indications to suggest that strong probability. Much of the reasoning that dwells on this probability is intuitive and is the result of connecting isolated items in one work or works, with other items similarly isolated in other works. This process, of intuitively connecting isolated events from works related to each other by the period and milieu in which they were written, weaves a pattern that becomes almost as convincing as would documents substantiating the dates and events themselves. This is particularly true in such cases where unfortunately the documents do not and probably never did exist. Hence we have in many instances only these intuitive insights to go by. Such insights can be useful when they follow the clues of events of culture and history and when they are compounded with the clues provided by the character of the people who moved in, and were involved with, the aspects of the culture and history that transpired within the confines of their own lives.

The recurrent visits between the royal families and the aristocracy of Spain and Portugal must have offered opportunities for the mutual contacts of the members of their retinues. In these retinues were probably Lucas Fernández and Gil Vicente (1465–1537?), the latter still considered in our day the greatest of the Portuguese dramatists. Born in Portugal, Vicente wrote his plays both in Portuguese and Castilian, the majority of them being in the latter language. Because of the probable relationships of a professional nature between Fernández and Vicente, some details of which will be needed in a later discussion, it seems advisable to allow some space here to the matter of their mutual acquaintance.

Fernández, as we saw in our preceding chapters, probably traveled to Portugal. The famous Portuguese scholar Carolina Michaëlis de Vasconcellos was among the first to give thought to Fernández' Portuguese journey. Mentioning him in connection with Encina, she wrote: "My suspicion that Encina, like Lucas Fernández, had been in Portugal, becomes increasingly stronger." [1] Inasmuch as the balance of her comment in this passage has to do with Encina rather than Fernández, we omit it as of little pertinence here.

As for the royal and aristocratic retinues that traveled between Spain and Portugal, we recall that the governments of the two countries were uncommonly close because of the political and familial bonds between them due to the successive marriages of King Manuel of Portugal with two daughters of Ferdinand and Isabella. Manuel first married the older daughter, Isabel, in 1497, and after her death in 1498 at childbirth, he contracted marriage with María in 1500. In the not infrequent royal family visits, many nobles' entourages, including that of the Duke of Alba, also took part. Both Fernández and Encina, who were simultaneously serving from about 1496 till 1498 in the household of the Duke, had ample opportunities to be included in the traveling suites. In Portugal they would have made the acquaintance of Gil Vicente, first a silversmith in the Portuguese court, then a royal entertainer.

Contemporary chroniclers give eyewitness accounts of the exchanging visits of the royal Portuguese and Spanish families. An important aspect of their descriptions is the attention paid to the role that Fernández' employer, the Duke of Alba, played in the affairs relating to the two countries. This serves as a guide to the whereabouts and travels also of one of his entertainers, Lucas Fernández. In the *Chronica do serenissimo senhor rei D. Manoel* (Lisbon, 1749), Damião de Goes relates the Duke's share in the reception made for the King of Portugal and his bride, Isabel, upon their arrival in Castilian territory. He also describes the ceremonies which took place during their visit to Toledo in the year 1498 where the young monarchs swore their vows as heirs to the crowns of Castile and León. It seems reasonable to assume that in the retinues of these royal and eminent families there traveled the three writers of our present interest, Fernández, Encina and Vicente, who thereby came to know each other.

A further reasonable assumption is that the Portuguese royalty and nobility, while being entertained in the palace of the Duke of Alba, enjoyed the productions of Fernández and other entertainers, and that Lucas probably composed for them one or more of his festive plays; the Portuguese king's silversmith-entertainer, Gil Vicente, coming in his suite to Salamanca would have opportunity to watch the performance. This then would afford a means by which the authors would have a basis for getting together, to talk shop, plan, discuss, eat, and drink as good fellows are wont to do.

It is of course probable that Lucas Fernández as well as other companions, such as Encina, would have appeared among the Duke's people during a reciprocal visit to Portugal, and that Fernández would have taken with him some play in manuscript to the Portuguese court where he would then present it. He could then have acted a part in the play personally, as could also have Encina, when they performed for the delectation of the King and Queen and their court. One such occasion may very well have been the wedding of María and Manuel in October of 1500 at Villa de Alcácer. The vows were actually pronounced by the royal couple on the thirtieth day of the month. It would not be strange if, during the wedding festivities that lasted several days, the first *Comedia (Comedy)*, composed *ca.* 1496 by Lucas Fernández, were presented as part of the varied entertainments on the program for the many guests that came to the wedding. It was an accepted tradition to present such a play at a wedding celebration, and the *Comedy* was particularly suited for the occasion, dealing appropriately with the topic of marriage.

The *Comedy* and probably other plays of Lucas would have been presented in the palatial halls of the Portuguese court, as were the plays of Encina.[2] It is possible that the author-actor even prevailed upon the local talent to assist him in putting on his plays. Gil Vicente thus would have had a good chance to become a participant. This was the type of apprenticeship he could profitably have served before becoming a writer on his own account. Fernández and Encina had gone through a similar procedure in their own literary development, as did most other dramatists.

We may suppose that the contacts that began early in the lives of the dramatic writers when they formed part of noble retinues led them to nourish these relationships for a time even after their service to their respective lords may have come to an end. Lucas, after leaving the ducal court at Alba de Tormes, found a receptive atmosphere in Queen María's palace. She probably had exhibited interest in his dramatic and musical ability, and perhaps it was she herself who officially introduced the poet-dramatist to the Portuguese court and was the one thereby to give an additional artistic impetus also to Vicente. The latter's first work, *The Herdsman's Monologue,* was presented in her honor two days after the birth of her first son in 1502. Though it seems that Queen María was the object of Vicente's adulation in his very first play, the plays that followed were inspired not by Queen María, but by the so-called Queen Leanor, sister of King Manuel, who strove to encourage Vicente in his career as a writer.

II *Further Data for the Fernández-Vicente Relationship*

The lack of documentary proof of personal meetings among some of the early Spanish and Portuguese dramatists necessitates the search for other reasonable means to postulate such events. One of these is the internal evidence in the works of the authors themselves that at times, coupled with historical and cultural events of the day—all intuitively combined—may provide the desired information.

As will be seen in Chapter 10 on Sources and Influences, Lucas Fernández' first *Comedy* served as a direct source of Vicente's second dramatic effort; this was the former's nativity play, *Auto pastoril castellano (The Castilian Pastoral Play).* The influence could have been as early as 1502 [3]—although Vicente admitted knowledge of Fernández' dramatic works only years after their publication—perhaps in 1536, but surely after 1521 and, of course, before Vicente's death in 1537. Vicente made this admission in a letter which appeared in the prologue to the *Copilação (Compilation)* of his works, published posthumously by his son, Luis, in 1562. The letter is directed to King John III of Portugal (reigned 1521–1557) in which Vicente spoke of *Os livros das obras que escritas vi* (The books of works that I saw written). In his letter Vicente confessed to familiarity with the edition of the *Farces and Eclogues* which Lucas had published in 1514 in Salamanca, but he makes no other reference to his knowledge of Lucas' works in manuscript, nor to having witnessed their presentation with his own eyes as an explanation of his early source material. Yet the unmistakable verbal similarities in the *Comedy* and *Auto pastoril castellano* (composed in 1502) argue for early acquaintance on Vicente's part with Fernández' play. The question of how he managed to learn of it is still something of a puzzle.[4] How can we explain Vicente's obviously thorough knowledge of the Fernández *Comedy* several years before its publication in book form? We can speculate that Vicente saw an early manuscript of the play (hardly an unusual circumstance in those times), or that, even though we have no documentary evidence, Gil Vicente may have seen Fernández' play performed while the former was on a visit to, or perhaps while a student in, the University of Salamanca.[5] Still a third option, one more in the realm of possibility, is that Vicente saw the play performed in the bilingual Portuguese court itself where he was serving in the double capacity as silversmith and entertainer—probably as a performer of a sort, perhaps initially as a part-time actor. He could even have played a role in Fernández' play and thus could have memorized portions of its lines which were later recalled in his own work. In the following paragraphs we will attempt to show that there was a strong likelihood, as one of Vicente's plays tends to reveal, that Lucas Fernández was present at the Portuguese court as an entertainer and that some of his productions were therefore accessible to Gil Vicente, who thereby became familiar with them. Vicente's pertinent play, the autobiographically rich *Auto pastoril castellano*, yields evidence that Vicente did indeed have opportunity to know Lucas Fernández personally, and consequently the latter's work as well, either through access to it in manuscript form, or as a spectator seeing it performed in the court of Portugal. It may be, as suggested above, that Vicente was an actual participant on the boards in the work of Fernández. A close examination of this particular work by Vicente illuminates, moreover, the mutual awareness, the personal contacts, and furthermore the friendships that existed among the three primitive peninsular dramatists: Lucas Fernández, Gil Vicente, and Juan del Encina.

It was Aubrey F. G. Bell who noted that the *Auto pastoril castellano* is among the plays of the Portuguese dramatist that have autobiographical touches: ". . . we may be quite sure," he wrote, "that the parts of the herdsman in the *Visitação*, of the mystically inclined shepherd, Gil Terrón, in the *Auto pastoril castelhano,* and of the *rústico pastor* in the *Auto dos Reis Magos,* were played by Vicente himself." [6]

As we examine the *Auto pastoril castellano,* we discover the following items of interest: (1) on the authority of Aubrey Bell, it is believed that the role of Gil Terrón is played by Gil Vicente himself; (2) it appears that the part of Bras is played by an otherwise unnamed but popular actor who on several occasions seems to have taken the role of Bras Gil in Lucas Fernández' *Comedy;* and finally, (3) the character of Lucas is probably played by none other than Lucas Fernández, who was apparently in Portugal either for the express purpose of presenting his *Comedy* at a court marriage (as suggested in the preceding portion of this chapter), or already employed, albeit on a semipermanent basis in Portugal, as an organist in the chapel of Queen María. This concatenation of circumstances would explain quite readily Lucas Fernández' recognized influence on Gil Vicente. Lucas may even have ignited the bright spark that induced Gil Vicente to try his hand at writing drama, if one bears in mind that there was likewise the immediate incentive created for the play by Doña Beatriz' personal request. [7]

How do we come to the three conclusions listed above? How do we draw the conclusion that Vicente and Fernández probably knew each other personally? First and foremost, we have the support for this thesis which is derived from the similarity of the proper names that exists between the characters of the play and the individuals who portray them. These names happen to coincide with those of the court entertainers Vicente and Fernández. Secondly, the support for our conclusions is derived from the fact that the author, Vicente, plays a role in his dramatic piece. In the same continuing tradition of the earlier actor-authors, like Fray Iñigo de Mendoza (*Vita Christi,* ca. 1482) and Juan del Encina, who acted in their own plays, Gil Vicente likewise enters directly on the scene to present his play. We can deduce this from the initial words of the piece which reveal that Gil Terrón [Gil Vicente] has found a "home" to his liking, for he says, "I want to put my things down here." In effect what he is saying is, "I want to make my home here." [8] Gil then proceeds to make revelations of his own humble background and his with-

drawn personality (*Vicente*, p. 9). All this has been accepted as
a reflection of Vicente's own life.

Further dialogue seems to be pertinent to Juan del Encina and
supports an exchange of conversation between Vicente and Lucas
Fernández concerning their mutual friend. Besides knowing
Lucas [Fernández], Gil [Vicente] also knew Encina well and
asks one of the companions about him: *¿Conociste a Juan Domado* [Juan del Encina] . . . ? ("Did you know Juan Domado
. . . ?"), (*Vicente*, p. 9, v. 52).[9] He expresses concern for Encina's
welfare, and Bras reports the following item concerning Encina:
*Anda, anda acompañado,/ canta y huelga en las majadas,/ que
este mundo, Gil, a osadas,/ ¡mal pecado!/ se debroca muy priado*
("He's still around with companions,/ he sings and has fun in
the sheepfolds,/ because this world, Gil, I dare say,/ the devil
be damned,/ comes to an end very quickly."), (*Vicente*, p. 10,
vv. 65–69). Encina, as we have already seen, left the service of
the Duke of Alba in a disgruntled mood four years before, that
is, in 1498, and upon failing to obtain the position of cantor in
the Cathedral of Salamanca, which was awarded instead to Lucas
Fernández and two other youths, he went to Rome by way of
Portugal.

With this discussion we are not necessarily trying to show here
that the *Comedy* influenced the *Auto pastoril castellano,* but
rather to stress the friendship, and the mutual awareness that
the Iberian Renaissance dramatists had of each other, and that
Lucas Fernández in particular had a hand in entertainments at
the Portuguese court. Vicente's play suggests that the *Comedy* of
Fernández was presented quite regularly at wedding celebrations
as attested to by the words that Gil addresses to Bras. Bras is
evidently played by the actor who represents a character by that
name in the *Comedy.* Gil [Vicente] directs himself to Bras, the
actor: *Tú que andas siempre en bodas,/ comiendo toros y vacas,/
¿qué ganas tú, o qué sacas/ de ellas todas?* ("You who's always
at weddings/ eating bulls and cows,/ what do you gain, or what
do you get out/ of it all?"), (*Vicente*, p. 8, vv. 29–32). Bras seem-
ingly belonged to what might be called a group, if not a complete
company, of actors and dancers, for Lucas [Fernández] seems
specifically to indicate members of the group when he cryptically
says that he has lost *dos cabras* (two goats), (*Vicente*, p. 11, v.
82), of his herd, and continues, *Perdiéronse por ahí,/ por la*

vega,/ o algún me las soniega ("They got lost around there/ in
the plain,/ or else someone is stealing them from me"), (*Vicente,*
p. 11, vv. 85–87). His "flock" went astray while, spellbound for
a couple of hours, derelict in his duty, he watched one of the
dancers from another "flock": *Nel hato de Bras Picado/ andava
María bailando;/ yo estúvela oteando./ Boca abierto, trespor-
tado,/ y al son batiendo el pie,/ estuve dos horas valientes;/
el ganado entanamientes/ ¡a la he! no sé para dónde fue* ("In
the flock of Bras Picado,/ Mary went around dancing;/ I was
looking at her/openmouthed, spellbound/ and tapping the rhythm with my foot,/ I bet I was there two hours;/ meanwhile the
livestock,/ by my faith,/ I don't know where it went"), (*Vicente,*
p. 11, vv. 88–96).

Somewhat more personal elements also come to the surface
as Vicente's drama continues to unfold. We learn that Gil [Vi-
cente] even feels confident and secure enough of his friendship
with Lucas [Fernández] to take the liberty of criticizing him.
This is brought about when Lucas shows by his speech that he
is resigned to the fact that what he has lost, as possible members
in his acting "company," is a lost cause and he merely philosophizes, *ya perdido es lo perdido* ("what's lost is lost"), (*Vicente,*
p. 12, v. 107). Gil thereupon proceeds candidly to chide him,
*Tú muy perezoso estás./ ¡Busca, busca las cabritas!/ Tras que
tienes muy poquitas,/ ño te das/ de perder cada vez más* ("You're
very lazy./ Go and look for the little goats!/ Since you have so
few,/ don't put up/ with losing more of them all the time"),
(*Vicente,* p. 12, vv. 110–14). There may be other important implications below the surface of this last phrase besides the allusion to the loss of actors. The phrase may refer also to his shaky,
imperiled status as director of the entertainment at the ducal
court at Alba de Tormes. By this time Lucas Fernández, as Encina earlier, seems also to have been losing ground at the palace
of the Duke of Alba; the reason therefor may only be conjectured.
He had, to be sure, obtained the position of cantor at the Cathedral of Salamanca, but something else in the way of privileges,
or fringe benefits, may have been taken away from him before he
finally became at least temporarily chapel musician for Queen
María in the Spanish-infiltrated Portuguese court.

In reading the *Auto pastoril castellano,* one is struck by the
notion that Lucas and Gil feel a certain comfortable comrade-

ship which allows each to rejoice at the success of the other. Lucas calls his companions over to share their joy, *Tomaremos gasajado,/ que Gil Terrón está aquí/ en abrigado/ allegre y bien assombrado* ("Let's enjoy ourselves,/ since Gil Terrón is here/ well taken care of/ and happy in his shelter"), (*Vicente,* p. 13, vv. 139–42). There is a detectable sense of joyous fellowship among them as they get together, for they feel like old friends who have common backgrounds and interests. For the moment, at least, in their snug little circle they do not let personal envy rear its ugly head. Silvestre, still another participant in the play, chances upon them and gleefully observes, *Ora terrible plazer/ tenéis vosotros acá* ("Well, you're all awfully happy around her"), (*Vicente,* p. 13, vv. 143–44). Not to be overlooked is the plain matter of fact that Bras, the actor, and Lucas [Fernández], the dramatist, likewise have a close personal relationship. This is brought out by the nature in which they refer to each other, namely as *amigo* (friend), (*Vicente,* p. v. 231), and *compañero* (companion), (p. 16, v. 234).

In the course of time, by mingling with people at court, Gil [Vicente] became surprisingly learned: This may imply that he did not necessarily have to attend a university to obtain his education, even though he came from a humble, country background. Bras says to him, *¡Gil Terrón lletrudo está!/ ¡Muy hondo te encaramillas!* ("Gil Terrón is mighty smart!/ You've come up a long way!"), (p. 24, v. 423), and Bras openly marvels, *Ya lo veo, ¡soncas!/ Quien te viere no dirá/ que naciste en serranía* ("Yes, I see, yes indeed!/ Who'd say just by looking at you/ that you were born in the hills"), (p. 24, vv. 424–26). In the next two verses, which form the concluding words of the play, we get a foreshadowing of what is to come after this performance. Lucas [Fernández] observes, *Cantemos con alegría;/ que en esso después se hablará* ("Let's sing with joy;/ because we'll have more time to speak of that later"), (p. 24, vv. 427–28). We may conjecture from the last quote that our dramatist is confident that the audience will doubtless hear more of his friend, Gil, as his renown grows.

Lucas Fernández' presence in the Portuguese court in 1502 is strongly implied by the text of the Vicente play written at that time. Such a stay there at that particular time would help to explain Fernández' influence that is so manifest in Vicente's

Auto pastoril castellano. Lucas Fernández, while staying in Portugal, probably presented his *Comedy* at the important marriage celebrations that would take place as indicated above. It may even be that this, the presentation of this play of occasion, was the principal reason for his going there in the first place. His acquisition of the post in Queen María's chapel, perchance as musician, is also probably related to his visits there.

We believe we have shown the strong probability that Lucas Fernández' presence in the Portuguese court had a decisively catalytic effect upon Gil Vicente. With Lucas' guidance and even probable participation in the first complete *auto* by Gil Vicente, the silversmith, sometime actor-turned-dramatist, received his momentous start. The similarities between the early works of these two writers can be more easily appreciated when the mutual awareness of the writers themselves is seen to be quite possible.

From all indications, Lucas Fernández was a well-traveled cleric, very much aware of the events in the world immediately surrounding him. He was not totally immersed in religion, but rather in life, almost to the same extent as were Juan del Encina, Bartolomé de Torres Naharro, or Gil Vicente. He was, moreover, a man of a large ambition for material security. He did not rest until he succeeded to a considerable extent in reaching goals that satisfied him. Ultimately he attained a respected academic position that gave him social distinction at the University of Salamanca. He had rubbed elbows with the great and the near-great in the Spanish and Portuguese courts as entertainer, actor, dramatist, musician, and organist. To these vocations we should add those of educator and businessman. His life's interests were broad in scope and he could often combine many of them successfully in some delicate balance. He was a complex and many-sided human being. His basic interest in drama was only one, but an important, facet of his polychronic personality. He published just one volume of his plays, but with it he sounded a unique and a remarkably lasting note.

CHAPTER 4

Corpus Christi Celebrations and the Early
Vernacular Theater

I *Theatrical Tradition. Its Acceptance by the Church*

IT may be helpful to devote some pages to a discussion of
Lucas Fernández' part in the festivities of the religious holidays mentioned in passing in the first chapter. We are once again
indebted almost entirely to the magnificent work of Dr. Ricardo
Espinosa Maeso, who compiled and published the documents pertaining to the poet-dramatist. But first, a brief review of the early
theater.

In Spain, perhaps as early as the tenth century, there had appeared certain dramatic performances in Latin, even as portions
of the church liturgy itself, although at times divested of their
popular elements. The quasi-dramatic snatches that were part of
the liturgy are known as "tropes." [1] This rudimentary drama
became very much a part of the Corpus Christi celebrations
which were first instituted by Pope Urban IV in 1263. [2] Some
literary historians have concluded that the tropes were forerunners of the Iberian drama which became the theater in the
vernacular tongues. It cannot be firmly shown, however, that the
Spanish popular theater had its beginning in the primitive dramatic form of the tropes and that it organically evolved by a
trial-and-error method to the formation of the full-fledged theater
of the sixteenth century. There is no way to disprove the existence
of a popular theater in the vernacular. Although manuscripts of
this earlier vernacular theater have failed to survive—excepting
a fragment of the twelfth-century nativity play, *El auto de los
Reyes Magos (The Drama of the Three Wisemen)*—it is difficult
to imagine the uneducated portion of the public that knew little
Latin doing without entertainment of a dramatic nature to accompany that provided by minstrels, acrobats, dancers, etc. As
education in the vernacular became more widespread, writers
grew more cognizant of the existence of a larger audience for the

longer, more serious type of drama, that previously had been traditionally restricted only to the more refined social circles. These circles of course had, as we know, enjoyed fine drama in the Classical languages that had endured for centuries. The Classical Roman and Greek theater was always present, and many manuscripts of ancient times, particularly of Terence and Plautus, were harbored, utilized, and performed by religious and university groups within the ceremonious halls of institutions of higher learning, of the churches and the cloisters throughout Europe in the Medieval Ages, and likewise during the ensuing Renaissance. The Medieval period was not so lacking in culture and the arts as we are sometimes prone to imagine. Latin or Neo-Latin plays appeared continuously throughout the Middle Ages until the vernacular came completely into its own and supplanted Latin as the sole language of both the popular and the cultured classes in most European nations.

The growth of the vernacular drama became most apparent in the conventional places for public gatherings, namely in the church, where a large portion of the public came to witness dramatic functions in religious ceremonies and on festive occasions. As understanding of Latin declined, so the vernacular theater supplanted the Classical dramatic productions and appropriated their audience while at the same time it attracted a new popular clientele by taking advantage of the willing audience in the church. At the very time we tend to hail the birth of the Spanish secular theater in Encina's brief one-act eclogues, and, similarly, the beginning of the Portuguese theater in Gil Vicente's *Herdsman's Monologue,* we already have a fully-developed play in Spanish which is so long in fact that it cannot easily be produced in one sitting before an audience. Consequently it is often placed in a category of a hybrid nature—the genre of the dialogued novel. This is the Classically-inspired play by Fernando de Rojas, the *Comedia de Calisto y Melibea* (Burgos, 1499), better known as *La Celestina.*

As previously suggested, for many reasons present-day scholars have come to question the heretofore widely held notion that "the beginnings of medieval European drama are to be found in the tropes of Christmas and Easter, written to ornament the liturgy, and sung in churches." [3] Rather, it appears closer to the truth to sustain the contrary view, that the Classical, the Medie-

[51]

val Latin, and the budding vernacular drama penetrated into the medieval religious services and thus gave rise to the tropes. Sister Mary Marguerite Butler very appropriately asserts: "The indisputable traces of the *comoediae elegiacae* and other classical models appearing from the first through the twelfth centuries are evidence that the classical writers never lost their appeal to the popular imagination." [4] Later this same drama of ancient origin was reflected in the sparse forms given it by Encina in his eclogues, as well as in the copious version of it produced by Fernando de Rojas.

While it is true that most of the earliest plays that we have on record in the vernacular are religious, it does not follow that secular plays in the popular language did not coexist; they may even have preceded the religious ones. We have only to cite the *juegos de escarnio* (mockery plays or plays of derision) which were censured by Alfonso X in the *Siete Partidas*.[5] The existence of secular drama alongside the religious is proved by Alfonso X's remarks. His disapproving attitude helps to explain the dearth of surviving texts of secular plays. The preponderant one-sided evidence of extant religious texts that give the erroneous impression that only religious drama existed in the vernacular is to be explained by the fact that texts were preserved best in the libraries of the religious cloisters. Copies of the secular plays rarely, if ever, found their way to the well-managed libraries, and hence were not preserved. The secular works were used, abused, discarded, and left to rot. There were few public or private libraries to conserve them. Religious libraries had no use for such secular works, and the chances are that they were quickly destroyed if they did manage to find a place in ecclesiastical libraries. Hence the rise of the false impression that the vernacular theater had its beginnings in the religious tropes, or, for that matter, that it evolved painfully from indigenous dramatic elements oblivious to the already highly developed form of entertainment as the Classical drama, the farces, mimes, mummers' plays, masques, etc. As O. B. Hardison, Jr. writes, "The existence of a strong, highly conventionalized vernacular tradition in the twelfth century raises a serious question about the dependence of later vernacular drama on the liturgical tradition." [6] At approximately the same time that Alfonso X speaks out against the "mockery play," there existed in Spain, as already observed, the anonymous

[52]

mystery play, *El auto de los Reyes Magos,* which may be dated as early as the middle of the twelfth century. In French the earliest bit of dramatic dialogue extant is the religious mystery play called *Le jeu d'Adam (The Play of Adam),* also an anonymous work, somewhat later than the Spanish play, dating from the end of the twelfth century.[7] The evident coexistence of a vernacular tradition both in the mockery as well as in the mystery plays supports the above statement by Hardison.

It is beyond the scope of this chapter to expound at length on the theories for the growth of the secular drama in Spain. But it may briefly be recalled that at least three major theories have been proposed for the appearance of the vernacular drama and should be mentioned. The one currently in vogue among Hispanists enlarges upon the research efforts into Latin tropes of the Mass by R. B. Donovan [8] and maintains that the medieval drama is the result of a direct evolution from the primitive tropes of the Mass. This is the theory we felt obliged to reject above. Another theory espoused by W. L. Grant [9] declares that the medieval drama grew out of the ever-present influence of the Classical drama, and that there was no "Darwinian" evolutionary process, as submitted by interpreters of Donovan, but rather an interaction of complex events, situations, and influences. The most acceptable theory of all, then, is the synthesizing one which is championed by Sister Mary Marguerite Butler and supported by O. B. Hardison, Jr. It admits the interaction of various forces on the theater and permits a complex situation to arise, rather than adhering to an oversimplified theory. The synthesizing theory accepts the interactive influence of Classical drama, the religious services, etc. This all-encompassing, unexclusive, and eclectic theory is by far the strongest one and in our opinion the closest one to the truth. It agrees with the concept proposed by O. B. Hardison, Jr. that the view of "both/and" rather than of "either/or" is the most sensible one to espouse.[10]

It can be sensibly acknowledged as a consequence that secular plays in the popular language of the Iberian Peninsula, or in Neo-Latin, coexisted with and even preceded the appearance of the tropes in the Mass; that, in fact, the development of the religious plays is a result of the extensive encroachment of the popular theatrical conventions. These, already in vogue and well established in the secular world, were merely transferred for application to religious ideas that had been contained in the brief thematic expressions of the trope. In other words, the dialogistic trope was born through the encroachment of already existing Medieval drama written in Latin into the enclaves of the church; and the Easter Play, for example, is merely the fuller penetration of the secular drama in Latin into a religious atmosphere.

II *Lucas Fernández and Corpus Christi Performances*

In past ages, as today, on Corpus Christi Day the cities and towns of Spain took on an enormously festive air. Women looked into old trunks and cabinets and took out gayly-colored tapestries and wall hangings, often embellished with coats of arms, and hung them on the balconies facing the streets. In the large imposing cathedrals, as in the case of that at Salamanca, the main chapel was decorated with hanging draperies and tapestries which were either owned by the parish or lent to it by the wealthy families of the city. The Duke of Alba had a rich and magnificent assortment of them. In the days of Lucas Fernández, wherever the religious procession passed that day the streets were covered with reeds, thyme, and cattails, and the walls and trees were adorned with bouquets of flowers and potted plants. There were representations of biblical episodes in which appeared individuals or mannikins dressed up appropriately to characterize the personages involved. The mannikins constructed by local artisans would be paid for from the treasury coffers of the parish. Such statuesque scenes with living or artificial figures depicting crowning moments in biblical lives or those of martyrs and saints were paraded through the town. In the Salamancan archives repeated references were made to St. Sebastián, accompanied by his executioner or one or two of the latter's aides in the procession. There would also appear the four apostles with flowing and luxuriant beards, and King David, who would play his harp, while the Holy Sacrament would precede them, borne ceremoniously by torchbearers. And finally, there would be lively groups psychedelically dressed in gaily-colored costumes to furnish the dancing entertainment in predetermined places throughout the city. They would execute their acts and programs of amusement which would be followed by brief one-act plays that made up the major repertoire for public attractions on most similar holidays.

[54]

The dances and amusements were normally planned, directed, and carried out by those of the local townspeople who happened to possess the interest, ability, and desire to fulfill such community obligations. Usually they were modest artisans, but this modesty often belied unusual talents for what we call "show business" today. The Church Council would enter into contracts with the artisans or other talented individuals for particular performances. After participating in the same capacity year after year for several years, some of these gifted people would become real experts in their projects or acts, so much so that some of them would be known in the city not by their proper name but by a name derived from their special talent. There was, for example, a Cristóbal Sánchez, a strapmaker by trade, who excelled in the *tordión*, reminiscent of the modern dance called the "twist," and he was so expert at it that he came to be known with the nickname of *tordión*, and with it he is referred to in the book of accounts: Cristóbal Tordión (Espinosa, p. 578).

The records for most of the Corpus Christi Days in Salamanca are incomplete. For some years they are detailed and extensive, while for others they are summarily superficial, and for still others they are either completely devoid of useful information, or are missing and irretrievably lost.

In 1501, the expense sheets from the Cathedral of Salamanca for the Corpus celebration indicate with precision the sums of money spent for the purchase of collars, bonnets, hoods, shoes, linen, and sheepskins for costumes, ribbons, and lace; a mask for San Sebastián, wigs for three shepherds, and a rented wig for the "saint," etc. All this was expended for the players in the piece which was prepared by Lucas Fernández. The nature of the expenses reveals that the presentation included a San Sebastián, three shepherds, a duke, and a judge. That the festivities on that day were of the first order is indicated by the fact that twenty-four gallons of superior wine were bought at a nearby town and brought to Salamanca. This was not all, since wineskins were also rented to store other quantities of local wine for the celebration. The ledger shows further items indicating payments to carpenters for the construction of a platform upon which the play was presented, and also litters upon which the church organs were carried to places where they were needed for the programs. The expenditures show that six youths were paid for conveying the organs from place to place. Music was provided for the plays and the dances which included a popular saber dance. The dancers were not only paid for their performances, but given meals as well. Sour cherries, chickens, and bread were among the items which were provided for the crowds that gathered. Although some of the food may have been given away outright or destined for consumption by performers and workers, quite probably much of it was sold to the general public.

The stage preparations included the services of a painter. He was also charged with fabricating the crown for San Sebastián. A gardener was engaged to bring two carloads of reeds to be strewn about the church and on the platform-stage. In this manner the illusion of a rural setting was created. The canon and a vicar of Alba de Tormes were also paid for bringing three drums for the accompaniment of some of the acts in the entertainment. Someone else was remunerated for hanging up the tapestries and curtains to decorate the church and its cloister for the different spectacles and possibly for setting up a stage for the performances. There were two men, one designated as a "Castilian," who played music on a *vihuela,* a violin-like instrument played either with a bow or by plucking the strings with the fingers. A swordmaker and his companion were paid for *juegos que fisyeron* (amusements which they provided).[11]

What part did Lucas Fernández play in the activities for the year mentioned above in the city of Salamanca? What may have been the plays or performances he prepared and presented for the townspeople? From the ledgers of the Church Council of the Cathedral of Salamanca, published by Espinosa Maeso, we learn that for the Corpus of 1501 a carpenter's apprentice made a pavilion, a rudimentary stage, or hut in which some shepherds were to execute their performance which was prepared by Lucas.[12] What did this amusement consist of? It appears to have been the first *Comedia,* the comedy that features Bras Gil and Beringuella.[13] It is recited by two shepherds, two shepherdesses, and an old man. Espinosa Maeso has determined this by extracting from the accounts for 1501 the information that there were three wigs needed for the "shepherds," two pairs of shoes for women, and three pairs of shoes for the men. The players for whom costumes were acquired seem to coincide with the five personae of the *Comedia.* To reinforce this contention, we would

like to point out that the term "shepherd" was at that time occasionally used as a synonym for actor: *pastores* (shepherds)
were the actors of those days, as exemplified by the plays of
Juan del Encina, Lucas Fernández, and Gil Vicente. Although
the play was written several years earlier (1496), it appears to
have been presented on various occasions, and this would seem
to be one of them. It may be that because the play was in repeated demand, Lucas decided finally to publish it along with
some of his other works. Evidently, he felt that it was worth preserving.

For the 1503 Corpus Christi celebrations which fell on the
fourteenth of June, tapestries were hung to adorn the main chapel
of the Cathedral. More than six bushels of wheat were bought to
make bread for the crowds. Some forty gallons of wine were
secured this time, and a wineskin had to be rented to keep more
of it on hand. Six baskets of sour cherries were purchased and
an unstipulated amount of sweet ones. Two carts of reeds were
ordered again, and this time the accountant stipulated that they
were to be spread on the floor of the church. Among the amusements we find mention of a group composed of several male personages and a lady, a dance group of *serranas* (mountain girls),
plus an additional *abto de lo[s] estordjones* (act of the twisters)
performed by several people. There was a pastoral performance
made and put on by Lucas Fernández.[14] This, once again, appears to have been one of his own dramatic pieces, but its identification is difficult. It might have been any one of the plays because all of them, save the last *Auto de la Pasión (The Passion
Play)*, deal with shepherds. Even the Nativity was sometimes
performed in the early Corpus Christi procession.[15] The program
was supplemented by a musical recital by three men playing their
lutes and rebecks before the *arca* (coffer) in the same way as the
vihuelas had been played before it two years earlier.[16]

The church organs used were carried by six men. Again there
were drums in the procession. Among the characters in the procession, this time only San Sebastián is mentioned, but we also
have the name of the man who played his part, Pedro de Toro,
who received five *reales* for his work. Of his costume only the
headdress, or wig, is specified, for it was rented. A painter was
hired for making the arrows which pierced the saint.[17]

There was an executioner in the play with San Sebastián. He

was portrayed by a certain Benito de Mayo, whose name has thus been immortalized in the account book. He received two *reales* for his share in the program.

The ledger for 1505 indicates explicit expenses for the *momos* (mummers). Their mummings or masks were combinations of dramatic scenes and dances in which the characters were masked.[18] Sometimes it appears that there was a mixture of living and inanimate figures in a sort of tableau. The mummers provided a favorite form of entertainment among the populace, the clergy, and the aristocracy, and they habitually performed at coronations, at oath-taking ceremonies, and at almost any other kind of official occasion. In 1467 a group performed in which Isabella, the Catholic, played a part on the occasion of the fourteenth birthday of Prince Alfonso, half brother of Henry IV and brother of Isabella. The performance was prepared for the event by Gómez Manrique at the request of Isabella. There were nine masked figures representing the nine muses, eight of which were dressed in feathered costumes, while the ninth, presumably Isabella, was dressed in a fur cape. Besides performing a dance, each member recited lines of poetry extolling the virtues of the prince and expressing hopes for his further personal and national success. Similar spectacles of dance and recitation extended to Portugal in the fifteenth century and are still mentioned around the middle of the sixteenth century by Diego Sánchez de Badajoz in his *Farsa del Sacramento*. The mummers are considered by I. S. Révah to constitute pre-Vicentine theater in Portugal.[19] In 1505 on Corpus Christi there also appeared "mountain girls" who probably did some singing and dancing. The musical accompaniment, however, was somewhat more ambitious this time than in previous years, if we can judge from the annotations made in the ledger. There were kettledrums, five trumpets, a harp, a rebeck, and two *vihuelas*. The festivities included a play entitled *Auto del dios de Amor*.[20]

Lucas, as an adept organizer, was that year placed in charge of the group that presented the saber dance. There is no indication that he was involved in the performance of any dramatic piece, either his own or anyone else's.

To assure good attendance at the festivities, a messenger was sent out to all the chaplains and priests inviting them to come to the procession. In the preparation we find the usual expenses for canvas, its tinting and sewing into costumes for the actor-dancers of the mummers. The consumption of good wine seemed to be increasing year after year. There was now a total of forty-four gallons of wine ordered from the nearby towns for the merry-making. Certain foods were also bought in larger quantities. Twelve baskets of sweet cherries were ordered and the accountant remarked that there were no sour ones available that year, thereby implying that they would have preferred the sour variety for their purposes. The consumption of bread declines, however. About five bushels of grain were ordered. The program once again featured the old standby, San Sebastián. A painter had the usual task of preparing some part of his costume. This time his staff needed painting, but there is no mention of any work required for his arrows or for his crown. As happened in earlier years, six men carried the organs to the spots where they were needed, but the locations are not specified. Then, the popular performer, Cristóbal Sánchez, was paid for organizing his specialties, a "small" as well as the "big" versions of the *esturdión;* the dance otherwise known by several renderings of the word—*estordión, turdión,* and *tordión.*

The list of expenses for the Corpus Christi holiday of 1508 provides considerable and unusually detailed descriptions of the preparations for the festivities. Some of the amusements entailed the appearance of three mummers and a lady who was noted to have worn brief clothes. There were also ten mountain girls and seventeen mercenary Swiss soldiers, as well as Negroes and a Negro woman who prepared a dance. This cosmopolitan atmosphere assumed the proportions of an international festival with the introduction of four Portuguese dancers who executed their steps to the beat of discs and tambourines. Their appearance is further evidence of entertainers crossing the borders of Portugal and Spain, which we discussed in the previous chapter in connection with courtly visits. Finally there appeared three peasants who presented the *abejón,* a rustic dance performed to the accompaniment of three small drums. All of these performers presented their programs on Sunday in the Cathedral, and after that they went through the city to present similar programs before the people in the streets.

A brief dramatic piece was also presented as part of the day's spectacles. It was listed as the *Avto de fortuna e el Rey e la*

Reyna e el hermjtaño con el pastor (Play of Fortune and the King and Queen and the Hermit with the Shepherd). The same musicians that performed in 1503 were engaged to play, and they, like the dancers, presented their program twice, first in the church and then in the streets of the city of Salamanca. The popular sword dancers were one of the standard attractions, as in earlier years, and they too performed twice in the day.[21]

Even more explicit and detailed was the orderly report of expenses incurred years later for the Corpus of June, 1531. Over a generation had passed since Lucas Fernández first took part in the celebrations, and some changes were bound to have taken place in such popular, annual displays which involved almost the entire province of Salamanca. Many traditional items were retained. We begin, however, to see a slight trend toward a more baroque taste, with more noticeable frivolities, the result perhaps of a less stringent code of religious ethics then in vogue. One of the traditional appearances was that of San Sebastián, but there also came a new saint, San Martín, to keep him company. The perennial theatrical rustics still performed their bits, and twelve sheepskins had to be ordered to make seven pairs of buskins and three pairs of boots for them. Their number, then, had increased by two from that mentioned for the 1501 play.

Character props, as the wigs made of dyed hemp, are still on the order list, and four beards were rented for the players who represented the four Evangelists. The young "rustic lads" with their customary gear were present to entertain, and similarly other youngsters were on the program to present dances. For the first time a bagpiper was employed to accompany the "Jews" represented in one of the pageants. The organizers of the festival dedicated greater attention to the smaller children and their diversions. Horses were made out of paper and brightly designed for them, while a dance was also organized in their behalf. The notes in the ledger suggest an apparently ambitiously pageanted representation of Heaven and Hell which was not only performed in the church, but also carted around town. White sheets were used as the trappings for Paradise, and shrubs and flowers were brought in from the hamlet of Tejares, just across the river from Salamanca, as stage props. Specific mention is made of the play as *Representación de Adán y Eva.* The recorder speaks of a wig for Adam and laments that it was temporarily mislaid. To make matters worse, he added with horror, too much money had been spent on it. To represent the evil serpent of Paradise which tempted Adam and Eve, a little boy was dressed up and painted appropriately. This play seems to have been patterned along the lines of the partial stage setting described for a Christmas play which was performed in Valencia in the fifteenth century.[22] Alongside of Heaven, Hell was represented in colorful detail with its devils, who stuck on painted oxen tails.[23] The demons covered themselves with dust and dressed in tinted coarse cloth from Anjou. Reeds were carted into town to be strewn on the church floor. We are told that the scenery and stage carts were prepared and constructed in the church itself, and the people employed for this had spent long hours in finishing their tasks on time. The carpenter, for example, worked for three days preparing scenery and background sets. On the eve of the celebrations, when they were running behind schedule, the workers remained late; and when darkness came, they worked on by the light of candles provided by the church. When they diligently worked extra hours into the dark night, making the final necessary preparations and putting on the last touches, they also required some special treatment. The invaluable account book shows that besides the expense of the candles, the people milling and bustling around the church, going about their business with an enthusiastic, holiday spirit, were given refreshments consisting primarily of bread and wine.[24]

A complying, experienced parishioner was placed in charge of arranging for the many dances. He obtained the services of thirteen people for one dance: six of them were Basques, six others were friars, and there was one Guinean. In another dance group there were seven rustic lads and three lassies who were shod in orange-colored boots. The dance master took it upon himself to provide the dancers' masks, to supply bagpipe music and to hire a drummer for the group. Besides his responsibilities of an artistic nature, there was also the very practical one of making sure there was enough to eat for his group of participants.

The procession was supplied with somber marching rhythm of the trumpets and the drums. Eight men rather than the usual six were required to carry the organs. One of the carts in the religious parade carried "King David" who sat atop it playing a harp.

For the crowd's repast, six and a half bushels of grain were used for making bread, and white wine was expressly brought all the way from Cantalapiedra by a muleteer. There were sweet and sour cherries for dessert, as well as cakes. A new note of affluence seems to have crept in: for the first time there is mention of ham at the meals.

The last entries in the account books of the Church Council which pertain to the Corpus are those that give some inkling of the amusements and games for the holiday in the year 1534. Plays were becoming more popular as there were at least three of them documented for the day: *Auto de los vizcaýnos* (*Play of the Basques*), *Avto de los yndjos y de los negros* (*Play of the Indians and Negroes*), and *Avto de los serranos y serranas* (*Play of the Mountain Lads and Lassies*).[25] This was complemented by the *turdión* dance, which had been imported from France, and, as its persistence testifies, had grown to be very popular in Spain in the sixteenth century.

Among the plays can be noted the presence of one that deals with what may be construed as very typical material of the day, a *Play of the Indians and Negroes*. The impact of voyages and discoveries to Africa and the New World was focusing some of the attention of the people on the expansive scope of Spanish national affairs. Church festivals served as a vehicle, or as an excuse, for the dissemination of all sorts of news, information, and propaganda.

III *Reaction against Church-Sponsored Performances*

Lucas Fernández died in 1542, but the expense accounts of his home-town church continue to hold further interest for the history of the theater. The notes for the Corpus Christi of 1550 do not contain any material that refers to Lucas or his works, but they are significant because they contain a brief item to the effect that an individual was paid to act the part of a *bobo* (fool).[26] The roles of the comic shepherds had by now been expanded to include "fools," a different comic type of the popular performances.

As time went on, the expenses of these festivities mounted, and the church income began to decrease. There were people in the second half of the sixteenth century in Salamanca who were daring to speak up against the performances of the *autos* and wanted merely to continue with the dances. There was even a growing insistence that the latter be really "good dances." Obviously in recent years they were of a nature that left something to be desired. Finally in 1562, the year that saw the death of Lope de Rueda, several votes were openly cast in the Church Council against the inclusion of the *autos*, albeit the majority was still fond of them and wanted them retained along with the dances. Eventually the Council decided that another *auto* besides the one to be presented by the choir children should figure on the agenda, but there was a word of caution added with respect to its contents, namely that the *auto* must not contain things that ought not be said, and that the things that will be said should be decent and the money paid for the play should be properly used (Espinosa, p. 406). This statement immediately awakens reminiscences of a similar pronouncement of the *Siete Partidas* by Alfonso X against the *juegos de escarnio*. A complete revolution in the theatrical public entertainment cycle of the Church seems to have been reached.

From the preceding notes it can be surmised that by the middle of the sixteenth century the comic, theatrical character was expanding to include the *bobo*, a successor to the humorous shepherd and also a forerunner of the later comic character of the Spanish stage of the Golden Age, the *gracioso*. The actor who played the *bobo*, as all the other participants in the public entertainment programs in years and generations preceding, received due payment for his services. These actors were not mere amateurs, but at least at times were professional performers. The growing importance of the theater is marred, however, by a note of dissatisfaction, verging on hostility, rising in the Church Council against the plays it considered to border on inadequacy and even on impropriety. We come to a rejection of those institutions that fifty years earlier had been clamored for and highly esteemed —the years that stimulated talented men such as Lucas Fernández and Juan del Encina and others to try their skill at preparing public entertainments. In the middle of the sixteenth century nothing seemed to be sacred to those involved with the theater, for pious sanctimony required a difficult discipline beyond the reach of most of the artists. The plays, it should be said in justice to ecclesiastical censure, had become licentious, scabrous, and in a sense decadent. They would be revived in their more cherished form only a generation or so later when Juan de la Cueva comes on the Spanish scene.

Even though our present concern has been largely with the Corpus Christi holiday, Lucas Fernández' role extended beyond it to other festive occasions, such as public celebrations of marriages, appointments to high offices, national events, and Christmas and Easter holidays. Indeed we can surmise that Lucas had a hand in planning, arranging, and carrying out many other church and university programs as well. His academic position was one that carried varied obligations with it. In January of 1546, for example, there is an entry in the accounts of the Church Council showing payment made to Lucas' successor in the chair of music at the University to cover expenses incurred in the performance of a play on Christmas Eve. Even before Lucas became a professor, he had written two plays specifically dealing with the birth of Christ—a fact which made these dramas highly appropriate for presentation at Christmas. No doubt he was called upon also to make similar arrangements for other Christmas seasons during his years of service.

There was cause enough, then, for Lucas Fernández during his lifetime to compose and produce plays for popular consumption, not only for parishioners and people affiliated with the University, but also for the general public that was interested in celebrating the diverse religious events. These helped to brighten their lives that were so often filled with stolid daily routines. The records of the Cathedral of Salamanca published by Espinosa Maeso reveal not only Lucas' contributions to the revelries of religious and institutional holidays, but also delineate the diversified forms of public entertainment then in vogue, the plays, tableaux, dances, recitations, music, and songs—in a word entertainments not unlike those that we enjoy today in our own varied spectacles.

CHAPTER 5

General Characteristics of
Lucas Fernández' Plays

I Versification

LUCAS Fernández wrote a song-drama and six *Farsas y églogas al modo y estilo pastoril (Farces and Eclogues in the Pastoral and Castilian Manner)*. They were all printed in Salamanca in 1514 and were reproduced in facsimile in Madrid (1929) by E. Cotarelo y Mori. Three of the six are profane, or secular, as is also the song-drama; one play is religious and two are semi-religious. The sequence of their appearance in the book seems to coincide also with that of their composition and is the following: (1) *Comedia (Comedy)*, (2) *Diálogo para cantar (Dialogue for Singing)*, (3) *Farsa de la Doncella* known also as *Farsa del Caballero (The Maiden's Farce* or the *Farce of the Gentleman)*, (4) *Farsa de Prabos* known also as *Farsa del Soldado (Farce of Prabos* or *Farce of the Soldier)*, (5) *Égloga del Nacimiento (Eclogue of the Nativity)*, (6) *Auto del Nacimiento (Play of the Nativity)*, and (7) *Auto de la Pasión (The Passion Play)*.

Each of the plays is preceded by a brief introductory synopsis, or *argumento* (plot summary), which also names the characters of the play in question. Except for the *Dialogue for Singing*, the *argumento* of which merely consists of a few words indicating its author, the characters, and also that the play is "based on [the song] 'Who made you, Juan, a shepherd?'" the briefest of the plot summaries, oddly enough, introduces the longest play, *Farce of Prabos*, which has 951 lines of text. The longest summary belongs to the *Play of the Nativity* which has only 629 lines. As an example from the text of a plot summary, here is a translation for the *Farce of Prabos* (*Farsas*, p. 97):

Farce or quasi-comedy, written by Lucas Fernández, in which four persons appear, namely: Two shepherds, one soldier, and a shepherdess. The first shepherd, called Prabos, enters as he suffers from love for a lass named Antona; while the said shepherd is cast upon the ground contemplating and speaking of his ailment, there comes a soldier; while he talks with the shepherd about his grief, the second shepherd, the third person, enters. He is named Pascual. The soldier has some disagreement with him and the other enamored shepherd makes peace between them. Later, Pascual, when he has learned of Prabos' love, calls the lass, and he [Pascual] and the soldier marry them off; they then go to town singing.

Each of the plays is written in verse, which differs more or less from play to play. The author refers to the verses of the *Farce of Prabos* (*Farsas,* p. 99) as *coplas,* a term that may mean not only "couplets," but any type of stanza the author may choose. In *Prabos,* the stanza is of ten lines. The first four form a *redondilla* (a stanza of four octosyllabic lines rhyming abba), while the last six lines are octosyllabic with the exception of two four-syllabled lines of *pie quebrado* ("broken foot"). The usual rhyme scheme of the final six lines is ccdccd. We offer here one of the stanzas for the reader's examination:

> *Ya ño quiero churumbella,*
> *los albogues, ni el rabé;*
> *alegría aburriré,*
> *pues huye de mí, yo della.*
> *Pues lo que busco, ño espero;*
> *lo que quiero,*
> *jamás lo espero de hallar;*
> *es mi dolor tan artero,*
> *que me muero*
> *sin saberme quillotrar.* (p. 99)

In his other plays, Fernández is more likely than not to use the stanza of four initial lines as in *Prabos,* while the six lines following may vary in some way or another from the *Prabos* stanza. Not all of the plays have stanzas of ten lines. Thus, the *Comedy* has only eight per stanza; they are octosyllabic with the rhyme abbaacca, while all the other plays have nine lines per stanza (except *Prabos,* as already indicated): the *Play of the Nativity,* the *Dialogue for Singing,* and the *Maiden's Farce.* The nine-line stanza is made up of octosyllabic lines with rhymes in abbaaccaa, abbaccdcc, and abaabcddc for the three plays respectively. The

Maiden's Farce furthermore differs from the other two by having a *pie quebrado* in lines four and eight.

López Morales sees in the poetic art of Fernández the influence of the verse forms used by the troubadours.[1]

We observe other incidences among the plays according to the similarity of their versification, particularly in the first four lines of the strophes, which are more uniform than are the remaining lines of each stanza. Thus the *Comedy* can be paired on the basis of versification with the *Play of the Nativity*, while the *Dialogue for Singing* goes with the *Farce of Prabos*, and the *Maiden's Farce* coincides with the versification in the first five lines of the *Eclogue of the Nativity* and of the *Passion Play*. All the plays are based mostly on the octosyllabic line and only the *Comedy*, the *Play of the Nativity* and the *Dialogue for Singing* do not contain the *pie quebrado* that appears in the stanzas of the other plays.

Lucas Fernández varies the rhyme scheme also in the *villancicos* (carols), or various kinds of songs he includes in his plays. Each play ends with a song or two, and there may be one or two within the play as well, though this latter practice is not uniform. In the majority of the songs, the basic stanza consists of seven lines varying between six and eight syllables to the line. A typical rhyme scheme is ababbcc. At the head of each song of seven lines there usually appears a three-line strophe which also apparently serves as a refrain to be repeated after each basic stanza during performances. The rhyme scheme in the refrains is fairly constant, dcc, and thus repeats the rhyme of the last two lines of the basic stanza. The versification is alike for two series of three songs each: the second song of the *Comedy* (*Farsas*, p. 74), the second of the *Maiden's Farce* (p. 96), and the first song at the end of the *Passion Play* (p. 176) are structurally the same, the first song of the *Maiden's Farce* (p. 94) and the first one of the *Play of the Nativity* (p. 153), as well as the second song of the *Passion Play* (pp. 176–78) are also alike in their versification. The songs in the *Eclogue of the Nativity* and in the *Farce of Prabos* are unique. The first has eleven octosyllabic lines to the stanza with the rhyme abbaaccdcec (p. 136), and the second has twelve hexasyllabic lines per stanza rhyming ababcddccddc (p. 119).

Fernández has scrupulously avoided placing two songs in the same play that would repeat the same rhyme scheme and that would contain the same number of syllables per line. When he writes two songs for the same play, he varies them not only in content and length, but also either in the number of syllables per line or in their rhyme scheme. This textual and structural variety probably reflected a similar variety of melody as well. It is to be regretted that at present we have no information at all about the melodies to which the songs were sung.

There are no *pies quebrados* in these *villancicos* or other songs. Songs in Latin and brief ones of three lines in Spanish appear only in the *Passion Play.*

II *Play Structure*

Lucas Fernández' plays and his song-drama, *Dialogue for Singing,* intermingle elements that reflect trends characteristic of what later would be labeled Naturalism, Realism, Romanticism, as well as religious dogma. All of these are found to a varying degree in most works of literature as reflections of various attitudes toward reality. Both the *Comedy* and the *Passion Play* by Fernández are exceptional pieces of his dramatic output, being balanced at opposite poles of the dramatic genre. The former, which was his first effort at drama that has survived, contains the theme of love treated in a realistic and rather comic way, while the latter, the last of his surviving plays, stems from a profound religious inspiration based on the Crucifixion. Situated between these two poles are the song-drama, which is inspired by the courtly love tradition, the two plays that concentrate on the parody of courtly, unrequited love, and the other two pieces that deal primarily with the theme of the Nativity, with interspersed pastoral episodes of comic tone. All of the plays are typical examples of early Renaissance drama in the Spanish vernacular.

Lucas systematically follows an easily observable plan in his plays. His initial scenes carefully prepare the audience for the action that is to follow. The technique is one of preparation for the story, rather than one of exposing the spectators to a sudden burst of an energetic sequence of actions that is typical of the device of *in medias res.* Lucas' approach is somewhat restrained. The introductory scenes skillfully introduce the audience to the "feeling" and the tone of the play. The initial speech of the first actor on the stage usually sketches the background mood for the events to unfold. By means of the dialectal speech—used early in all plays but the *Passion Play*—with its coarse words and jocular nature, the spectators are made aware of impending buffoonery. They are assured early that there will be an intrusion of mirth and laughter into a performance sprinkled with some tones of melancholy, sober philosophy, and some religious dogma. Dogma is present to some degree in every one of the plays except the *Comedy*. The *Passion Play* is distinctive in lacking comic devices. Its tone is established by the very first lines which portend tragedy: "Hear my grieving voice," and by the high level of the tragic tone which is sustained to the very end: "how could they have/ killed their Maker?/ —Ay, for you, sinner" (Translated [Lihani] from *Farsas*, pp. 157, 176).

The general plan that Lucas Fernández uses for the first three plays of the princeps edition hinges on a simple central plot, intermittent comic relief, a happy ending in marriage, and a conclusion with a song and dance. The song-prelude to the concluding dance expresses an optimistic, cheerful tone.

After the introductory, mood-setting speech of each play, including the comic, the farcical, the semireligious, and the religious, the conflict begins to unravel with the approach of characters who pit themselves against the protagonist, or sometimes against each other. This permits the dramatist to introduce a variety of effects that produce humor or pathos, and to implement other dramatic devices before he carries the action to a final reconciliation between the contending parties. A song-ending, a feature in all the plays, is an integral part of Lucas' dramaturgy. If there are less than four actors on stage, they summon a friend or two from the wings to make up a quartet for a polyphonic rendition of the lyrics. The last lines usually seem to invite the audience to participate in the singing. There are thus at the conclusion of the plays normally four characters on stage who are essential for the song routines. They may enter into the events as needed by the plot, but when they are summoned on stage at the last moment, they are of little significance to the action. In addition to the song in the *Comedy* and in the *Play of the Nativity*, there are explicit stage directions that make it clear that the dramatist placed emphasis on the ensuing dance as well. The ideas expressed in the songs are usually optimistic. This no doubt accedes to the note of optimistic revelry that the audience typically awaits on festive days of public entertainment and merrymaking.

Into the basically skeletal plan presented above are brought detailed variations of whatever theme the play may have. In the secular plays the theme is that of unrequited love. Its depiction as a chronic, physical ailment gives the author a chance to satirize medical treatments. Moreover, the earthy emphasis on realistic, physical, often purely animalistic desire parodies the detached affectation of idealistic courtly love.

The same structural design is followed for the semireligious plays on the Nativity in which the conflict begins at the appearance of the second character on stage when he clashes with the protagonist. Their struggles are interrupted by a friend who announces to them the birth of Christ, whereupon there is an exchange of repartee during the course of which the significance of the sacred birth is explained. The play concludes with a joyful note of faith in man's ultimate redemption.

The birth of Christ is treated as a current event, where the demarcation between historical fact and contemporary life is obliterated, and the historical event acted out in contemporary surroundings becomes a living reality. The author thus rejects a normal chronological order of events, and prefers to exercise some liberty in the use or adaptation of biblical history. This is not unique to Lucas Fernández, nor, for that matter, to Spanish authors, but characterizes medieval European theater in France and England as well. We can appraise Fernández' fine skill in handling small, bare incidents, based on just a few words from the Bible, to which he gives knowledgeable shape, light, and substance until each moment of the past, powerfully caught and held in a descriptive imagination, briefly belongs to the present.

The song-drama, *Dialogue for Singing*, falls into a category by itself, and is merely a sung dialogue on unrequited love. Also of its own distinctive genre is the sacramental play dealing with the Crucifixion, in which is played a vivid forceful narration of the drama at the foot of the Cross. There is no real character who plays the crucified Christ, for the Crucifixion itself is already history and is relived only in the minds of, and in the words narrated by, the participants. At first a single character enters on the scene and soon another joins him; a conflict ensues, though not between the two of them, but rather together with them, that is, they are in harmonious agreement, as they face frightening supernatural conditions that cause them to wonder anxiously about the state of the world. There is, then, an inward psychological conflict prompted by the Crucifixion which torments them. The denouement comes when the distressed players, seeking consolation, finally find it in the concept of the resurrected Christ, symbolized by the tabernacle containing the Sacred Host. The resolution is achieved by their vicarious adoration of the Lord as they kneel before the Host, somewhat on the order of the reverence given the Infant Jesus in the Nativity plays.

Fernández normally keeps his stage continually occupied and concentrates the action in a single place. Therefore, he tends to maintain the three Classical unities, although there is considerable lack of restraint in the free use of time and space. The unities, then, when observed, achieve this as a natural result of the limits of action within which the single-act plays are conceived.

There are at times rather precipitous personality changes, so as to permit quick, happy endings. There are, as already suggested, many glaring anachronisms, the result of telescopings of time, which are intentional and at the same time conventional. For example, saints associated with a community are invoked for a play's presentation simply because the local inhabitants expected to see their favorite saints appear among them on festive occasions, though such saints may not have experienced any real association in their lifetime with the historical event which Fernández through his imagination presents to his public.

Lucas displays a certain sense and need of dividing his dramas into scenes. Concerned with one-act plays, he makes no formal scenic divisions of them, but often provides careful, explicit stage directions throughout the plays from the first *Comedy* to the last work, the *Passion Play*. Lucas surpassed his contemporaries in the use of these explicit stage directions. He avoids brusque unannounced appearances of characters on the stage by usually having other players already on the scene summon the others to come on stage. There are no particular problems posed by the staging of his plays, no unusual technical devices, such as pulling a star on a string across the Nativity scene, or having "flying men" appear. Although Lucas speaks of supernatural events, he has them take place offstage, though mechanical devices to make them happen on the stage itself were not unknown in his day; in fact, sophisticated multiple stages existed, and were a common phenomenon in the Medieval religious plays which were a synthesis of spectacle and didacticism.[2]

William C. Bryant has correctly observed that Lucas Fernández' plays have a well-advanced structure and contain themes and techniques which later become basic to the fully developed drama of the Golden Age.[3] And G. Cirot states that as far as realism and movement are concerned, Lucas was superior to Juan del Encina, and that in the *Passion Play* he surpasses Encina in the emotional impact of the words he uses to convey the impression of that transcendental event.[4] His plays, in their fundamentals of the dramatic art, are as up-to-date and current as are love, laughter, and tears, revolving as they do around the common human themes of love, honor, and religion. The comedies are little gems that depict customs and manners, since in them are often to be found the rustics at their ordinary daily tasks, making comments on their normal chores, on their games and diversions, on their family and ancestors, and on their loves and prejudices. These humble shepherds are very much alive and very human, even in their comic moments which may tend toward farcical proportions, but not quite reaching the abnormalities of stereotypes, and even the lesser characters like the hermit, Macario, and the Soldier have distinctive traits that give them individuality.

Even when two of Fernández' plays present characters with no specific baptismal names, thus having to be identified merely by generic terms like "soldier," "gentleman," "shepherd," they are nonetheless as complex as if they were given individualized Christian names. Coming during the transition between the Middle Ages and the Renaissance, Lucas Fernández was understandably an ambivalent writer who skillfully managed to weave both splendid entertainment and lucid instruction into his plays. His admirable mixture of these purposeful elements was one of the mainstays of his success as a sixteenth-century dramatist.

III *Artistic Use of Languages*

In the pages devoted to the general characteristics of Lucas Fernández' plays belong some comments on language. Fernández' use of language was peculiar in the sense that, alongside the normal Castilian language, he also resorted to the use of a rustic dialect, especially when he represented the common folk of his Salamancan region in several of the plays. Much could be said here about his language from a phonological, morphological, lexical, and stylistic point of view; but rather diligent and thorough studies have been published on the subject or are awaiting publication, and those must suffice. We will therefore merely skim the surface of the topic here.[5]

It is significant that Lucas Fernández injected into the title of the collection of his plays the descriptive phrase "in the pastoral and Castilian manner and style." In his sacramental drama, the *Passion Play,* we find the so-called Castilian style in exclusive use, while in the earlier plays an interlacing of both standard Spanish and dialectal pastoral jargon is present. Such mingling of popular with elegant speech increases the effectiveness of each in the process of character delineation and in the creation of comical interludes. Inasmuch as dialect tends to exist devoid of rules, which on the other hand conspire to uniformize the expressions of a country's standard speech, inevitable inconsistencies crop up in dialectal usage—inconsistencies which are perfectly admissible. Such differences and inconsistencies serve to reinforce the authentic nature of dialectal representation accorded to the regional speech found in the plays of Fernández.

Lucas had a profound knowledge of life, as it was lived in the province of Salamanca, through his sustained contact with people of different social classes. As a result, he was able to interweave throughout his plays the songs and dances that derive from the heart and soul of Salamanca. He could specify the towns from which his shepherds came, and he did so: Ledesma, Almuña, Val de Villoría, Rubiales, San Bricio, Doñinos, Gontinos, Vico-Nuño, Navarredonda, and Mogarraz. He was adept at handling their dialects. Although the standard language was more malleable, he found the local speech more forceful, more direct, and less assuming—less splendid, perhaps, but more entertaining to the spectators.

In order to comprehend the distance which separates the usage of language between the shepherds and the cultured people of the city in the plays of Lucas Fernández, one has to view side by side the speech of the shepherds and that of the gentry in the *Maiden's Farce;* that of Macario, the hermit of the *Eclogue of the Nativity,* as well as that of all the speakers of the Easter drama, the *Passion Play.* One can easily appreciate the unusual care placed by the dramatist in the exercise of the dialectal possibilities for theatrical purposes. He observed the speech habits later to be cultivated by Bartolomé de Torres Naharro, who was also very meticulous in his apportionment of speech among characters representing different levels of society. In brief, the language varies in accordance with the social classes exemplified by the protagonists on stage. Lucas assigns his characters the mannerisms which distinguish them within the social ambiences in which they moved. The vocabulary used by the cavalier and by the soldier, for example, is more refined than that utilized by the shepherd, and similarly the speech of the city damsel is more delicate than that of the shepherdess.

With the exception of the *Passion Play* the plays are written with a profusion of dialectal terms taken from the language spoken in the Salamancan region. This dialect is properly called *charro,* but it has come to be known in literary criticism, due to a confusion of terms and characteristics, as the *sayagués* dialect. This term, by the way, which has become a catchall, is used loosely to designate any and all Spanish dialects and corruptions of Castilian employed by sixteenth- and seventeenth-century dramatists for humorous purposes. Since it is a general term, it also encompasses the term *charro,* which designates the popular Salamancan dialect that was the basis for the humorous language employed by both Lucas Fernández and Juan del Encina. It was an incorrect identification with the district of Sayago in the southwestern region of Zamora that gave the dialect its misnomer of *sayagués.*

In the case of Fernández and Encina, it is possible to establish and identify the dialect they used as *charro* on the basis of the town names in the province from which their shepherds claim their origin. This dialect eventually degenerated, under the pens of later dramatists, and with its absorption of diverse elements —archaisms, deformed Latinisms, and pseudo-Latinisms in a conventional system—it survived in a conventionalized literary form to the very last years of the Golden Age.[6] It became, however, an impoverished dialect that was formed on the basis of a distorted idea of nonstandard speech, and retained only a few *charro* forms that were projected into normal Castilian. The *charro* speech is characterized by the palatalization of the initial *n* into *ñ* as in *ños, nos* (we) and *l* into *ll* as in *llabrar, labrar* (to work); the aspiration of the initial *f* producing *h* as *huerte* for *fuerte* (strong), *hue* for *fue* (was, went); the variation of endings in the plural form of the second person: *-ás, -áis; -és, -éis*, as in *mandás, mandáis* (ye command), *traés, traéis* (ye bring), etc. (indeed, *-és* and *-éis* are often found to be in rhyme); the plural imperative of the second person terminates in *-y* (which is, incidentally, the normal form in modern Portuguese): *anday, andad* (go, walk), *miray, mirad* (look). This imperative ending coexists with the standard form *andad*, as well as with an apocopated form *andá*. Sometimes the same apocopation is similarly found in the nouns such as *maldá* for *maldad* (wickedness). There is constant textual vacillation in the verbs *do, so, vo, estó* with *doy* (I give), *soy* (I am), *voy* (I go), and *estoy* (I am) respectively.

Furthermore, the rustic Salamancan idiom is characterized by rhotacism, i.e., changing a sound to [r]. A lateral sound [l] changes to an [r] if it is preceded by an occlusive, *p, k, b, g,* (but not by *t* or *d*), or by a labiodental fricative *f*: *placer* thus becomes *pracer* (pleasure), *blanco* becomes *branco* (white) and *flaqueza, fraqueza* (weakness).

The old forms of the future tense are prevalent in the *Farsas: terné, tendré* (I shall have), *vernán, vendrán* (they, you [pl.] will come), and the consequent conditional *vernía, vendría* (I, you, he would come) etc. The pronominal form *ge* (to you, him, her, them) still appears in standard usage in the early part of the sixteenth century, while the rustic shepherds were using the more popular counterpart *se* in their dialectal speech. *Haber* (to have) rather than *tener* (to have) is used to express the idea of possession, while *tener* is on occasion used as an auxiliary instead of the modern form which prescribes *haber* for this function. In keeping with the older forms of Spanish, we find the *r* of the infinitive assimilated to the following *l* of the pronouns as in *dezillas, decirlas* (to say them), *vella, verla* (to see you, her, it).

In reading the text for rhythmic purposes, it is necessary to make use of the synalepha repeatedly, and throughout the plays the emphatic form *a la he* (by the faith) is usually pronounced in two syllables, probably omitting the vowel of the middle word for syllable count, while the possessive adjective *mía*, when preceding a noun, appears as a monosyllable, losing its final vowel in pronunciation.

In addition, besides the few dialectal characteristics noted above, there are several terms which are seen frequently in the phraseology of the shepherds. There are such terms as *par, por* (by), *senor, señor* (sir),[7] *soncas, por cierto* (indeed), *asmo, creo* (I believe), and *quellotro* (that other) with its verbal derivatives, *perllotrar, llotrar, quillotrar,* which are *muletillas* (crutch or catchall words) changing their meaning according to the exigencies of the context, but which today are no longer in use.

There are frequent apocopations, particularly of the final *e* in verbs as *vinier* for *viniere* (will come), *cal* for *cale* (behooves), *vien* for *viene* (comes), etc. On a comparative basis of the dialectal language practiced by Lucas Fernández and that found in the *Coplas* appended by Cotarelo y Mori to the *Farsas y églogas* in his facsimile edition, we have concluded in a separate study that the *Coplas* should not be attributed to Lucas Fernández.[8]

In the works of Lucas Fernández a living segment of the true Leonese dialect is seen in full bloom, that is to say, we see in his writings the true representation of the dialect spoken at the turn of the sixteenth century in the region of Salamanca. It was Lucas who provided a firm linguistic basis for what had been an inexact, theatrical portrait of the language, as it was then existing in such works as the *Coplas de Mingo Revulgo,* in those of Iñigo de Mendoza, and in Juan del Encina. For this Lucas used the typical characteristics of the Leonese idiom as it pertained to the Salamancan region. Encina had not really allowed himself in his works to use the plebeian jargon fully, in spite of the fact that he knew it well. In his clever play, the *Auto del repelón,* there is decidedly a greater emphasis on true Leonese expressions. The play, as we pointed out, differs greatly from any other known to have been written by the pen of Encina, and as a result there has been some doubt expressed as to his authorship of it.[9] There is truly no Renaissance or Golden Age author who can compare with Lucas Fernández in the accurate depiction of the rustic colloquialism of the Salamancan province, nor in his intense and prolific use of it.

To what extent did Lucas know the towns about which he wrote? Lamano y Beneite suggests that Lucas visited all the localities he names in his plays, either in his role as a priest, or during periods of vacations or on family visits. By these means he was able to acquire a first-hand knowledge of the dialect he utilizes in his farces and eclogues. His superior and adroit portrayal of the prevailing patois of the common folk has long been recognized: "There are passages in the *Farsas y églogas* of Fernández that characterize him with a Salamancan provincialism that is much more correct than that for the other poet of the *Cancionero* [Encina]." [10] Menéndez Pidal had also noticed that Fernández used a language much "more properly rustic" than Encina's.[11] We know through comparison with modern studies of the Leonese dialect, as that done by Menéndez Pidal, that Lucas was a more precise dialectician than was Encina. In fact, the only comparable dialectal work of Encina's corpus of literary works that can parallel Lucas' is the *Auto del repelón*, but it is precisely for this reason—for its profusion of dialectal terms—that Encina's authorship of it has been questioned, and the possibility that it might be Fernández' work has been raised. Other subsequent popular dramatists like Lope de Rueda, Lope de Vega, and Tirso de Molina produced different versions of the *sayagués* dialect. For these and others who perpetuated the jargon, it ultimately became a mere literary convention, a stylized comic device, which consisted of a conglomeration of dialects, archaisms, popular expressions, distortions, and corruptions of Castilian.[12]

Lucas Fernández accentuated the realistic tendency of the age through the use of elements of the shepherd's earthy, sometimes uncouth, vulgar, and sensual idiom; but along with this, there is a grace and facility of language practiced by Lucas which adds a luster and beauty to the sundry peregrinations and conventional scenes that he unfolds. Lucas asserts himself as a natural poet of natural people who go about their daily habits and tasks. As elements of literary technique, he employs images, similes, and metaphors of visual and synesthetic, as well as of tactile and auditive implementation. His characters, whose love is unfulfilled and who are crushed under the weight of their despairing emotions, vent their feelings with references to nature's marvels: *Montes, montañas, boscajes/ secarse han con mi pesar,/ . . . / Las fuentes dulces, sabrosas,/ darán agua de amargor./ Las flores y frescas rosas/ olorosas/ no ternán color ni olor* ("Mounts, mountains, thickets/ will dry with my grief,/ . . . / The sweet, savory springs,/ will give bitter water./ The flowers and fresh/ scented roses/ will have no color nor fragrance"), (*Farsas*, p. 90, vv. 357–65). But hope springs eternal in the young heart, and scorned love in the very nature of things will in time be provided with a change: *La luna llena y crescida/ ¿no l'as visto ser men-*

guada?/ La nieue fría y elada,/ ¿no l' as visto derretida? ("The full, waxed moon/ have you not seen it wane?/ The cold and freezing snow/ have you not seen it melt?"), (p. 103, vv. 261–64). Along with lovers' sorrowful wailing is the pastoral tender language metaphorically applied to the Virgin: *Es rosa entre las espinas,/ . . . / es frol de las crauellinas,/ olor de açuçenas finas* . . . ("She is a rose among the thorns,/ . . . / blossom of the carnations,/ scent of the fine lily . . ."), (p. 135, vv. 551–54). The strongly expressive language, also present, can be savored in the following evocative tones: *Rompan, rómpanse mis venas,/ y riésguense mis entrañas/ con plazer, pues que las penas/ son ya gloria, y las cadenas/ libertades muy estrañas;/ buéluase mi voz de hierro/ y de pregón* ("Let my veins burst, let them burst,/ and let my entrails tear/ with pleasure, since pains/ are now glory, and chains/ very strange liberties;/ let my voice turn to iron/ and become a herald's [voice]"), (p. 132, vv. 431–37). The varied natural atmosphere is augmented by the vivid allusions to nature: *Hora muy huerte llentío/ haze aquesta madrugada./ ¡Rabia, y quán terrible elada!/ Juro a mí, que haze gran frío* ("It's a shivering cold/ we have this morning./ Gads, what a terrible freeze!/ I swear it's bitter cold"), (p. 139, vv. 1–3). *¡Ay de mí triste! ¿Qué aré/ por aqueste escuro valle?* ("Woe is me, wretched one! What'll I do/ in this dark vale?"), (p. 81, vv. 1–2).

With these examples we close the explanation of the artistic use of Fernández' language and of some of the general characteristics of his plays.

CHAPTER 6

Farsa de Prabos y el Soldado
(Farce of Prabos and the Soldier),
1497-1499

IN this chapter we shall consider the third play written by Fernández. It was his latest and best effort in the secular direction. Other plays were to follow in a more religious vein.

This play begins with a declaration by the youthful shepherd, Prabos, of the afflictions and tribulations caused by love among the young rustics. The play appears to owe something to Juan del Encina's *Égloga representada en requesta de unos amores*. Both Encina and Fernández place a pining shepherd in essentially the same predicament, one which expresses basically the same idea of impending death brought on by love's heartrending trials. But by now the theme of love is also as much Lucas Fernández' as it is Encina's, for Lucas also had treated it earlier in his own way. In the text of the drama he mentions several of Encina's plays, thus revealing his indebtedness to his mentor, but he likewise makes specific allusions to some of his own works. The express mention of these shows that his own production was sufficiently well known to the audience to be singled out for comparative purposes.

It is to four of Encina's eclogues that Fernández refers in his text. One of the eclogues appeared in 1496 in Encina's first *Cancionero*. A later eclogue by Encina that is a sequel to the one just mentioned, and in which the same characters appear, does not seem to enter into Lucas' thoughts as he writes his play. Two others were published in Encina's *Cancionero* of 1509, while the fourth was published as a separate fascicle and bears no date. What specifically are the plays by Encina that Lucas refers to? They are the aforementioned *Égloga representada en requesta de unos amores* of 1494, *El triunfo del Amor* of 1497, the *Égloga de Fileno y Céfira*, which appeared later in the *Cancionero* of

1509, and finally, the *Égloga de Febea* which was probably written in 1497 and published separately without any date. In the
Farce of Prabos and the Soldier, Fernández cites his own first
play, the *Comedy,* which we date as of 1496. The general interrelationships of works is not limited merely to the ones we have
just indicated; there are resemblances in Fernández' plays to
earlier as well as to later works of other authors.[1]

The story of the *Farce of Prabos and the Soldier* is as follows:
Prabos, which is a rustic form of the name Pablos, begins by com-
plaining of an incurable illness which afflicts him. While he is
meditating about his sad frame of mind, a soldier (named gen-
erically Soldado) appears. His first words reveal a cold haughti-
ness toward the shepherd as he addresses Prabos with "Hey, lad,
I mean, shepherd!/ What are you doing there all stretched out?/
lying in that meadow,/ woolly, snout-nosed, and uncouth?" (*Farsas,* pp. 99–100, vv. 101–4). But soon he becomes interested in the
causes of the shepherd's grief and in a sincere effort to help him.
Upon verifying that his incapacitation is due to love, he suggests
a cure, and compassionately turns to calling the shepherd "companion, farmer, lad," encouraging him toward recovery from his
ailment. The soldier's character arouses sympathy as he further
generously invokes the Almighty to restore the shepherd's health
(p. 103) and to guard his vigor and youth. He is after all a soldier
of the Faith, for he bears a cross on his chest, "So that it will give
us light" (p. 112, v. 602), as he later explains to Pascual, a second shepherd who comes on the scene.

Prabos mentions shepherds and maidens from former plays by
Encina and Lucas Fernández who were smitten by love: Fileno,
Céfira, Pelayo, Cristino, Febea, Bras Gil, and Beringuella. The
Soldado constrains himself from mentioning Trojan and Roman
lovers, for they are far too many to mention.[2] Pascual, the second
shepherd, begins mischievously to tease the soldier, while recom-
mending medicines to Prabos—medicines which are named for
humorous effect, for Pascual himself had used them to cure his
she-ass. (It is not clear at this point whether Pascual may have
been responsible for a play on words here, and referred thus to
his girlfriend or wife.)[3] The Soldado feels compelled to explain
the malady of love to Pascual and then to define to him the meaning of love itself. Thereupon, Pascual and Prabos join in cynically
degrading the soldier's way of life, while the latter feels obligated

to defend his profession: "We don't do so much harm/ that we
don't do some good,/ for we have well besieged Great Jerusalem" (*Farsas*, p. 108, vv. 450–52), which is also a reference to
the latest Crusades to the Holy Land against the Turks. When
he is scored for stealing shepherds' girls, he merely counters with
the excuse that soldiers are also human. When the Soldado
finally becomes so provoked that he angrily threatens to beat up
Pascual, Prabos obligingly steps in to pacify them, and lest they
forget his suffering, he reminds them that he needs their consolation. He then admits that the object of his affection is Antona.
Very opportunely she is sighted in the distance and is summoned
while they try to convince her that her love should be given to
Prabos. Succumbing to their arguments, she agrees to love him
with the condition that he convince her of his sincerity, marry
her, and stay true to her. Prabos is only too happy to comply, and
they are summarily married on the spot by Pascual, who assumes
the duties of a priest. Pascual's naive role-playing as a priest is
not a put-on to victimize the lovers, but is rather a role of momentous convenience that satisfies the desires of the betrothed,
who thereupon consider the marriage a binding one. And quite
legally so, as the *Siete Partidas* makes clear.[4]

Pascual directs the informal ceremony by saying, "Now, quickly,
quickly, join/ and hold/ your hands in sacrament" (*Farsas,* p.
117, vv. 804–6). When they do as directed, he announces, "I
marry you, I marry you/ even though I'm not a priest" (p. 117,
vv. 810–11), and calls for the exchange of vows: PASCUAL. "Do
you accept, Antona?" —ANTONA. "I do accept." —PASCUAL. "And
you, glutton?" —PRABOS. "I'm also happy/ to be her husband"
(p. 117, vv. 812–15). Then Pascual concludes the ceremony with,
"I give you my blessing" (p. 117, v. 816). The soldier who wit-
nesses the procedure then sententiously states to Prabos, "May
your cares be at rest/ and your griefs decreased [since] your
wishes are fulfilled" (p. 117, vv. 820–23). Finally, Pascual announces: "And we shall make the marriage/ public to all the
people" (p. 118, vv. 870–71). The marriage will thus be made
official through public announcements, and all the shepherds from
the surrounding area will come to drink and dance at the celebration. The soldier tarries to witness their newly found joy, and
the four characters join in a song on love. The *villancico* presents
a spark of hope for disdained lovers: in due time the hardest

heart will soften as does the ripening fruit on the tree. The song ends on an optimistic note prescribing faith and hope, instead of despair, in matters concerning love.

Of the four characters in this play, the Soldado stands out as the strong, dominant one, whose tolerance and wisdom guide the action to a happy conclusion in marriage. He is its guiding light, and as such he uses a language which befits his somewhat experienced, cosmopolitan outlook. His Castilian stands apart from the farcical and rustic dialect of the shepherds. Although his profession is not held in high esteem by those he meets, he remains a good example of the better members of the armed forces who did the fighting during the time of the Catholic Kings.

This play, the longest by Lucas Fernández, extending to some 951 lines, contains a correspondingly greater variety in content and a more extensive dialogue than do the others. The repartee between the Soldado and Pascual over the soldier's weapons, dress, and purpose, is not an integral part of the primary action, but holds interest as a depiction of provincial ideology. It reveals the country folk's negative attitude to the adventurous soldier's life, "That's a life of lazy ones/ that's a life without law;/ you do not fear God nor King;/ you go around like rascals;/ shameless and without conscience" (*Farsas*, p. 107, vv. 420–24). Some of these soldiers were mercenaries, as was the *soizo* (rustic for *suizo*, "Swiss") here described. Nevertheless, the *soizos* were reputed to have had a high sense of honor and justice.[5]

The shepherds, who dominate the activity on stage, are of a realistic type and besides their dialectal speech they are supplied with the traditional pastoral musical instruments, such as the rebeck and flageolet. Indeed, these instruments are already found well established in popular literature of centuries past, as in the *Libro de buen amor,* whose probable influence on Lucas Fernández we have already noted and will consider in greater detail in the chapter on Sources and Influences.

It is clear that ecclesiastic inspiration is not a basic tenet of *Prabos.* Instead, we have a comedy of manners presented with an illusion of an outdoor scene located in a meadow. Lucas excelled as a painter of idyllic scenes, combining country language with evocations of nature, as some of the early lines of this bucolic scene suggest: "O mountains, valleys, and hills;/ o, meadows, rivers, and springs,/ my senses have I lost" (p. 98, vv. 51–53).

There is a reference in the play to *esta otoñada* (this fall) which may suggest that the action takes place in late fall or early winter, possibly at Christmas.

The author gives a double category for his drama, calling it "farce and comedy" (*Farsas*, p. 97), which could be explained by the fact that the play has farcical overtones at the beginning and gradually leads to a happy ending which is typical of comedy.

In this play the playwright uses the theatrical device of false accusation as part of the cause of the mounting conflict among the characters. He had used it earlier also in his first play, the *Comedy*, in which the false accusation is perpetrated by the grandfather against his granddaughter whom he condemns for being ungrateful to him and for having acted improperly with her lover. With this he combines the false accusation of her sweetheart, Bras, for allegedly having deflowered the girl. In this *Farce of Prabos and the Soldier*, the accusation is founded on the general concept of a scoundrel soldier. Pascual shamelessly accuses the specific soldier he meets of being unworthy of the shepherds' trust: "Don't trust him/ . . . / for there's no trusting a hound" (*Farsas*, p. 104, vv. 303–4). In both cases mentioned here, one involving Beringuella and Bras Gil, and the other the Soldado, the accusation is unjustified, and after the wrangle, the real truth comes out and the imputed wrongs are rectified through apologies and redeeming actions.

The episodic slapstick scenes in the *Farce of Prabos* spring from the depiction of local manners and customs; they belong to a type of *entremés*, or short farce, popularized later as an insertion between the acts of a longer play. Particularly is this the case of the episode between Pascual and the Soldado. It becomes a picaresque incident which enters into the plan of the play without undue disturbance of its action, and indeed blending very well into it. The author takes advantage of the incident in order to arouse, divert, and entertain the public, dramatizing the ridiculous moments the soldier faces with the shepherds who are unfamiliar with his clothes and weapons.

PASCUAL. Well, and this snare, what is it?
SOLDADO. This is a halberd (*alabarda*).
PASCUAL. What d'you say, mister, packsaddle (*albarda*)?
SOLDADO. A halberd (*alabarda*) it is, fool.

LUCAS FERNÁNDEZ

PASCUAL. And this here?
SOLDADO. It's a dagger.
       And what a dagger!
PRABOS. Maybe, a muleteer's club?
SOLDADO. It's a manual weapon.
PRABOS. It looks more like a muleteer's axe.

(*Farsas,* p. 111, vv. 580–89)

To the shepherd, the soldier seems to go about dressed like a
monkey with "uncovered buttocks." In reality the fighting men
wore protective armor only in front, thus never daring in retreat
to turn their backs on the enemy. This fashion of dress was considered by the soldiers as a reflection of their bravery, and thus
served as a source of pride to them.

Such scenes as this one with the soldier are highly ludicrous,
but mostly because of the presence of the rustic. The latter considers himself equal to what were generally thought of as his
superiors. He may even believe that he is more worthy than his
lords, yet without decreasing the respect and affection that he
traditionally holds for them. Because he can laugh at the defects
and beliefs of those of whom he speaks, his own little peculiar
ways of gossiping, fighting and petty arguing favorably predis-
pose the audience to him. In addition to the social contrast between the soldier and the shepherd, a certain amount of satire
of the mercenary militia and to some extent the reincarnation of
the classical *miles gloriosus* (the boastful soldier) is present, as
Alfredo Hermenegildo and H. López Morales tell us.[6]

The scene in which the boastful soldier is satirized begins when
Pascual comes on stage. It covers slightly more than one fourth
of the lines of the encounter between Pascual and the soldier.
Pascual at first does not notice the soldier, and he begins talking
to Prabos. When he finally notices the soldier and excuses himself
for ignoring him at first, the soldier gets off on the wrong foot by
insulting him, calling him a *matiego* (one raised among the
reeds). This then leads to an exchange of insults, jokes, and an
argument between the two that lasts for more than a fourth of
the lines of the entire play. When the shepherd refers to the
soldier as a *perrigalgo* (hound), the latter retorts with "villain,
bastard, brute" to the shepherd, and makes it clear to him that
he is really angered. The shepherd is unintimidated: "So you're
mad at me too" (p. 105, v. 310). Prabos comes to the soldier's

defense and cautions Pascual not to pretend to be the soldier's equal. But when Pascual suggests the medicines he has used for his she-ass as a cure for Prabos' malady, the soldier can't contain himself and once again insults him for having said "A thousand foolish things" (p. 105, v. 337). The soldier then explains to Pascual that his friend's ailment is due to love.

There then follows a definition of love in which Pascual shows his naiveté by asking the color of love (p. 105, v. 381), and upon learning that love is Cupid, he resolves to let such a youth go to the devil. When he credulously wants to see Prabos' wound that was dealt him by Cupid, the soldier once again offends him with *puto tuerto* (one-eyed bastard) (p. 107, v. 398). By this time, Pascual is impressed by the soldier's explanations on love and concedes that he knows more than the priest. However, when he verifies that this wise man is a soldier by profession, he sees him in a different light again and exclaims that "It's a joyless life with rare pay" (p. 107, v. 417). Pascual continues with hints at a bit of social protest as he emphasizes "and you dare to steal,/ and to rob,/ and to eat by other people's sweat of brow" (p. 108, vv. 444–46). In the ensuing exchange (pp. 108–9), the soldier is impugned for being blasphemous, avaricious, greedy, lustful; yet not once is his bravery questioned, nor does he show signs of cowardice, a trait which traditionally goes with the boastful soldier of earlier literatures. This soldier listens tolerantly to Pascual's accusations and surprisingly is reserved in his own defense to which he comes on five different occasions. He maintains that they are not all that bad, or they wouldn't have a redeeming feature, like conquering Jerusalem; although they pillage lands, they do sustain justice; and if no girl escapes them, it's because they too are human; and if they take mountaineers' girls, it's because love knows no bounds; and finally if their occupation is one of cursing and blasphemy, he is convinced that anyone who believes strongly, also curses in the same fashion.

Yet the main intent of Fernández in this passage seems to be to present the typical, boastful, swaggering soldier. This he does for the first time on the Spanish stage, as we know it, inasmuch as the swaggering soldier of the *Celestina,* the Centurio, appears only in the expanded version of the drama which is dated 1502, while Fernández' work is believed to be between 1497 and 1499.

In a rather teasing and tongue-in-cheek manner, the soldier

attempts to intimidate the shepherd by threatening him with all
sorts of lethal violence. These turn out to be empty threats, for
he does not harm a hair on the shepherd's head, and the latter
stands his ground, taking all the threats very lightly; in fact he
has fun responding to the soldier with new challenges to incite
him on to more ridiculous threats: "I'll turn you inside out" (p.
109, v. 501), "I'll slap you so hard you'll spit out teeth for ten
years" (v. 505–6), "I'll debone you piece by piece" (v. 511),
"I'll wipe the floor with you and cut you to shreds" (vv. 520–21).
He is surprised that the shepherd keeps calm and merely digs at
him with "what nonsense" (v. 513), and "You won't get a finger
of mine" (v. 519). When the soldier claims that the shepherd
already is in the jaws of death, his bluff is called as Pascual
utters, "To hell with the braggart" (v. 539), whereupon the
soldier's wrath becomes real, and as his blood begins to boil,
he shouts exaggerated threats like "I'll throw you so high you
won't fall down in three years" (v. 552). Pascual, unperturbed,
tells him to cool down, and when he resumes his further threats
and Pascual still dangerously plays the game of egging the soldier
on, Prabos finally steps in and reminds them he needs their help
and urges peace between them. The soldier then tells the shepherd not to be afraid, a superfluous comment, for he surely is not.
The shepherd then admits: "I was only joking" (v. 573), and the
two declare their new friendship. But even as friends, the shepherd, Pascual, still mocks the Soldado's dress and the latter explains its designated function, until Prabos again bemoans the
fact that they have forgotten his misery, whereupon they concentrate on helping him and fetch Antona to have her marry
Prabos.

The braggart soldier treated by Lucas Fernández on the
Spanish stage differs to a considerable degree from the *miles
gloriosus* of the Classical comedy. The latter brags about bravery
in incidents that he never participated in, and when his bravery
is actually to be tested on stage, he reverts to his innate cowardice. Fernández' soldier is a braggart, to be sure, but not about
his past exploits. He speaks in the plural when he points out the
virtues of his profession: "we besieged Great Jerusalem," "we
defend justice," and "we are also human." His bombastic threats
made to Pascual are so farfetched that neither the simple shepherd nor he can take them seriously. Lucas is indeed parodying

the boastful mercenary with the exaggerated threats made by the Soldado, but the latter has made them as a sort of game himself. He is not a blustering fool. Pascual provokes him and, in fact, baits him on to make a joke of it all. Pascual is the one who teasingly says, "You must have killed a hundred," while the Soldado agrees, "They're so many, there's no counting them." Then Pascual makes the joking remark, "I bet they were lice." (p. 110, vv. 531–33).

In the first phase of the repartee, it is the shepherd who gets the better of the Soldado, but the role switches when the soldier explains his armament. The terms are unfamiliar to Pascual and while he attempts to mock the soldier, he is in reality mocking himself. At the mention of the cross on his breastplate, the Soldado becomes philosophical and avoids becoming a burlesque caricature, as he explains that the Cross gives him light and "the entire world is subject to it" (p. 112, vv. 602–3). With one more jocular comment in which the soldier's cap is called a helmet, the contest ceases and focus turns once more to Prabos and his complaints. The soldier becomes an important participant in the play's denouement.

The cowardice of the *miles gloriosus* of Plautus' comedies is thus absent here, as is also that of the scheming Centurio of the *Celestina*. Lucas Fernández' soldier is a unique product. Unlike Centurio, he has many virtues: he is a man of letters, wisdom, kindness, and justice, as well as of warlike accoutrement. The aspect of braggadocio identified later with the braggart soldier is more in character with the Caballero of the *Maiden's Farce*, but even there Lucas Fernández' inherent tolerance of various types of individuals is sufficient to curb the desire to ridicule anyone bitterly, and the courtier, too, has his redeeming traits of kindness and understanding when he finally declares in the *Maiden's Farce* that he will respect the shepherd and be his friend henceforth.

In the encounter, Fernández presents two points of view—that of the poor peasant, and of the indigent soldier. He does this in an entertaining way so that the interlude adds a considerable note of light comedy to the play. It is significant that there is no slapstick or beating involved here, as there is in many other comedies of the time and later. It is, on the contrary, on a higher plane of humorous word exchange, puns, and sportive merriment. Lucas thus shows innovative imagination with regard to the characterization of the braggart soldier. Although the type is not known in Encina's theater, he is well defined in our present play.[7]

Joseph E. Gillet, without knowing the date of composition of the Fernández play, stated that possibly Fernández was influenced by the *Comedia Soldadesca* written by B. de Torres Naharro and published by him in Italy in 1517.[8] However, Gillet felt that the date for the *Soldadesca* was about 1508–9.[9] Under those circumstances, it is clear that since Fernández' play is earlier (1497–99), whatever influence there may be in the depiction of the soldier type and his life, such influence went from Fernández to Torres Naharro.

The two elements that have been seen to stand out in this play are (1) the local color, and (2) love. The play presents what is traditionally termed the formal definition of love. Although the lyrical element is expressed more or less in conventional terms prevalent during the epoch and reflecting sentiments and situations common in Encina's eclogues as well, Fernández displays a formidable lyric talent as he gives the vital emotions on this universal sentiment. The author explains that "Love is a transformation/ of the one who loves into the beloved;/ where the beloved is transformed/ by affection into the lover;/ it is the weight placed in balance,/ it is a level which makes two things into one" (p. 106, vv. 361–67), and ". . . this love in the heart/ is born and grows and sprouts/ and flowers in desire,/ and its fruit is affection" (vv. 371–74). "Cupid is a boy, a child and blind;/ and he is of a beautiful face;/ he casts arrows of fire/ without ceasing/ and always wounds in treachery" (p. 106–7, vv. 385–89).

For his time Lucas Fernández was an ingenious artist who knew how to present palpable, vibrant life through his writings.

CHAPTER 7

Secular Plays

THE two secular plays, the *Comedy* and the *Maiden's Farce,*
deal with daily matters which are lightly caricatured through
the actions of the simple shepherds. Both deal with the theme of
love. The second of the two contrasts the grace of an elevated
courtier and the charm of the lowly shepherd in their wooing
of the maiden. The *Comedy* deals with the same universal theme
of young love, but strictly on a rustic, anticourtly plane. Fernández shows the peculiarities of love, whether it is nourished within
the coarse attire and by the uncouth manners of the somewhat
sensual farmhand, Bras Gil, of the *Comedy,* or whether it glows
in the breast of the refined and courtly gentleman of the *Maiden's
Farce.* Even though the object of love be a humble peasant girl
like Beringuella (of the *Comedy*), the dramatist develops the
niceties and attractions of even the ordinary, common woman
which are the equal of those of the highbred, romantic damsel
of the *Maiden's Farce.*

The female characters in these two plays include the country
lass who is a woman of much common sense, and at the same
time both valiant and timorous. Lucas depicts her convincingly
as a marriageable damsel, fearful and uncertain about her immediate future, while she is searching for security. The solution
to her dilemma lies in a happy marriage relationship—a marriage
that would not be disturbed by financial problems or by the lack
of material things. She may be goaded and enticed with trinkets
and trifles, but she does not fall easy prey to her pursuer. She
manages, through the impressive use of a strong, independent
will, to attain her cherished goal of marriage.

To counterbalance the fine, virtuous, exemplary character of
the sophisticated courtly damsel of the *Maiden's Farce,* the author
provides earthy characters. Such characters speak and live with
the most candid and uninhibited immorality, but they possess a

certain ingenuousness of sentiment which, united with an atmosphere that is generally wholesome, makes their somewhat unrestrained and occasionally scatological language tolerable.

In these secular plays, Fernández presents a love which is not characteristically Platonic, nor idealistic, nor of a purely Christian character, but rather a love that is down to earth and realistic, a love into which enter elements of physical, sexual attraction and ideas of a materialistic nature pertaining to dowries and wedding gifts. The love is usually portrayed by the author as a normal, ordinary one that is found in various walks of life. Lucas generally concentrates on the physical and material aspects of it, thereby indirectly producing a rustic parody of the Platonic, idealistic courtly love of the aristocracy. The aristocracy had been known to affect disguises of a pastoral let's-pretend-type of milieu in hopes of reaching the idealistic passionate form of love with which it desired to escape the humdrum realities of its own life.

These plays contain simple, straightforward action unencumbered with complicated events. Yet, these are plays of kinetic, rather than static, drama.

I La Comedia (The Comedy), 1496

The *Comedy*, which is the first play in the princeps edition of 1514, is full of movement and constant animation. As Fernández' title indicates, it is classified simply as a "comedy," but for further precision it is sometimes identified by the names of its enamored protagonists, Bras Gil and Beringuella. The background for the scene is rustic, situated among crags and bushes, and the stage is busied with a constant state of activity. There is little narration of events that take place offstage. The characters are only five in number, but they are numerous enough to lend a suspenseful conflict to the love theme in which the burlesque, rustic element predominates. The humble, coarse, at times crude attempts of an uncouth shepherd at courtly love, that had traditionally belonged to a refined fairyland atmosphere, could cause easy hilarity before the aristocratic audience of the palace, and before the dandies and common people of the city. The play could be presented in the cloisters of the church just as easily as in a plaza in front of it, or at any neighborhood square in spite of its crudity and exaggerated rusticity. The comedy is concerned with a genuine love that ends happily in the marriage of two

young lovers. It may therefore be classified as a "marriage play"—
a play of occasion—and was suitable for performances at wedding
celebrations. It was probably presented at the marriage festivities
of important people, both in Castile and in Portugal. There are
indications that this play, although it was written in 1496 while
Fernández was an entertainer in the ducal palace in Alba de
Tormes, was also presented in Portugal, possibly at the marriage
of Manuel I to María, one of the daughters of the Catholic Sovereigns, and that it was performed again in Spain in 1501, as the
records researched by R. Espinosa Maeso suggest (Espinosa, pp.
406, 574).

At the outset of the play, we find the shepherd, Bras Gil, be-
moaning his accumulated agonies which spring from unrequited
love. Thereupon, his beloved, the haughty and scornful Beringuella, appears on the scene. After his impetuous revelations to
her of his discontent, really his first declaration of love to her,
she blandly advises him to take various medicines to effect a
rapid cure from his sufferings. The cures she suggests, however,
involve purging and are not of a nature to ease his mental anguish. Undaunted and unintimidated by her indifference and
frivolous abuse, he presents her with a trinket and a spoon as a
gesture of love. This "courtly" act, together with his repeated
complaints of suffering on her account, precipitates a sudden turnabout in her. She changes from distant, intractable disdain to
warm, intimate affection as she condescends to love him and
presents him with a piece of cloth, a favor which drives him to
ecstasy—distantly akin to Calisto's delirium with Melibea's sash
in Fernando de Rojas' *La Celestina*. The two then joyfully and
much in love begin singing a popular song, a *villancico*. But they
are abruptly surprised by Beringuella's grandfather and Gil's
master, Juan Benito.

Enraged at finding his granddaughter in what he considers
compromising circumstances with the young rustic whom he has
brought up as a servant, Juan Benito's first impulse is to attack
Bras Gil and give him a severe beating. On second thought, he
decides to punish the youth by taking him to court. A bitter
quarrel ensues in which the overly zealous Bras Gil and his old,
hot-tempered master exchange insults, a procedure known as
echarse pullas. They alternately threaten each other physically.
Fortunately, Miguel Turra, a wise shepherd of some education

which prompts him to quote Latin passages, appears as the arbitrator: *Calla ya, y callad vos;/ y veamos entre ños/ esta ryña por qué fue;/ y amigos os haré* ("Be quiet now, and you too;/ and let's see among us/what this argument is all about;/ and I'll make you friends"), (*Farsas*, p. 69, vv. 396–98). He then prudently dissuades Juan Benito from the lawsuit, saying that only lawyers would profit by it. Instead, he counsels him that by far the best solution to the problem is to let the two lovers marry. Juan Benito stubbornly objects to a marriage on the grounds that Bras Gil's social status is not equal to that of Beringuella. This insult to his family incites the youth to expound proudly on his ancestral lineage, which in reality is of course quite humble. But after hearing the description of Bras' family tree, Juan Benito realizes that he is well acquainted with the youth's grandmother, and is then ready to agree to the marriage. Willing even to make it more attractive to Bras, Juan enumerates the items of the dowry, a complete line of household furnishings for the new couple. The eager groom-to-be is in turn urged to recount his contributions; these consist of several domestic items which he will present to his bride.

Miguel Turra then summons his wife who simultaneously congratulates and teases Beringuella on her marriage. Juan Benito meanwhile philosophizes about the fleeting nature of youth. The play ends optimistically with the formalized betrothal of the two lovers performed by Miguel Turra, which is as binding as is marriage itself (as we have seen in the case of Prabos and Antona, Chapter 6, note 4). When Bras Gil and Beringuella indicate their consent to marry each other, Miguel Turra observes, "There's no need to say more,/ since both of them are happy;/ for by their mutual consent/ they cannot leave each other," and grandfather Juan Benito quickly adds, "Neither leave each other, nor even separate,/ according to the marriage laws" (*Farsas*, p. 71, vv. 481–86). The betrothal or an actual marriage on stage is an ancient dramatic formula which became common practice in the drama of the later Golden Age. There follows a spirited song which exhorts the actors, and indirectly the spectators, to join in a dance. The presentation concludes with the actual dance itself.

This first play by Lucas Fernández was probably composed around 1496,[1] for it appears mentioned in the *Farce of Prabos and the Soldier* (*ca.* 1497-9), as we have noted in the preceding chapter. It was most probably presented several times thereafter, including a showing on the day of Corpus Christi in 1501. It is a play in which the author's predilection for ecloguelike material is fully revealed in the masterful reflections of country life and descriptions of rustic love and lovers. In his discussion of the play, H. López Morales has noted that the treatment given the shepherd is realistic with a tone of rude sensitivity.[2] The shepherd who opens the play with the lamentations over the cruelties of love expresses ideas in pastoral rhetoric: "I curse Love./ To fire and to the devil with you./ I blaspheme at it and I curse it/ with great anger and furor;/ for its grief/ will not let me rest,/ nor even to breathe,/ showing me in this way its disfavor" (*Farsas,* p. 59, vv. 1–8).

Bras Gil finds earthy and rustic similes the most appropriate to describe his love for Beringuella: "I go about like a dog after the bitch,/ or the cow after its calf" (pp. 59–60, vv. 22–23). Later, when he describes the havoc that Beringuella's spurning has caused him, he says: "Food, it's impossible to eat;/ sleep does not descend on me./ Like a lamb suffering from gid/ I'm filled with anxiety" (p. 60, vv. 33–36). There are nonetheless lyrical elements present, particularly in the *villancico,* which depict love in the midst of nature: *En esta montaña/ de gran hermosura/ tomemos holgura./ Haremos cabaña/ de rosas y flores/ en esta montaña/ cercada de amores;/ y nuestros dolores,/ y nuestra tristura/ tornarse ha en olgura.* ("In this mountain/ of great beauty/ let's take joy./ We'll build a cabin/ of roses and flowers/ in this mountain/ surrounded with love;/ and our griefs,/ and our sadness/ will turn to gladness"), (pp. 64–65, vv. 216–25).

The *Comedy* has three-dimensional characters who are strong-minded, exercising their own free will, and molding their own destiny. They are not mere playthings of nature nor of capricious gods, and as a result the differences and conflicts that arise among them stir the action and arouse interest. This is a skillfully-constructed, sensitively-written, well-balanced production possessing sound literary and dramatic value. It contains lucidity of expression along with graphic language. This marriage-play, as heretofore observed, was destined to provide entertainment at weddings, particularly of notable people, being performed on those occasions by a troupe of well-paid actors.[3]

Inasmuch as the *Comedy* is a wedding play, its players are

about as risqué and free in their use of earthy language as are Torres Naharro's rustics under similar circumstances. In Torres Naharro's *introitos*, the rustics make sensuous remarks to encourage fertility for the celebrated marriage, and at the same time to strike the proper note of gaiety, mirth, and hilarity for the ritualistic event at which they are, after all, serving as entertainers. Lucas Fernández preceded Torres Naharro in using erotic expressions on a vulgar plane as Juan Benito questions the young couple: "What branch of sexual desire/ is between you here?" (p. 65, vv. 259–60). He asks his granddaughter: "Tell me, tell me, what happened?/ Tell me if he laid you?" (p. 66, vv. 269–70), and then turning to Bras Gil, he blusters: "Come here, you'll swear/ in the hands of a jury/ if you deflowered her" (p. 67, vv. 313–15).

This type of language with its raciness precludes lyricism from the scene, but it fits in with the burlesque intentions of the author to make fun of the unrealistic courtly love of the old and popular tales of chivalry.

Through the character of Miguel Turra, Lucas Fernández also heralded the appearance on the Spanish stage of the mediator to an argument in much the same way that Lope de Rueda (d. 1565) brought in Aloxa, the neighbor, to pacify the family of his *Paso de las aceitunas*.

II Farsa de la Doncella (The Maiden's Farce), *1496–1497*

The play, known also as the *Farsa o cuasi comedia (Farce or Quasi Comedy)* of the Doncella, Pastor and the Caballero, or *Farsa del Caballero (Farce of the Gentleman)*, is one of the oldest published plays in Spanish bearing the label "farce." In the fourteenth century the term was used in Aragón to refer to the canticles which were sung at the conclusion of the matins on Maundy Thursday. The word appears to have been of Old French origin from where it spread to Spain. Its use in Spain to describe a type of dramatic piece, however, seems to be a tangential derivation from the ecclesiastical usage in Aragón.

In this play the theme of love is developed in three or four successive scenes which take place in a setting outdoors near a roadway. A little variation creeps into the recitation on the cruelties of love through a certain romantic affectation in the complaint and lamentation of the Doncella—a complaint which contains considerable lyrical force. In spots, the play also possesses certain subdued farcical overtones, but because they are somewhat restrained, the play, in spite of its title of *Farsa*, retains the primary characteristics of less exaggerated comedy.

Only three persons take part in this play. It commences quietly with the Doncella nobly but aimlessly wandering through a dark valley in search of her beloved, the Caballero. Her path crosses that of a Pastor, who at first sight becomes deeply enamored of her and spiritedly tries to convince her to transfer her affection from the man of the palace to himself. He tries to convince her that he is a competent shepherd who excels in the rustic accomplishments of jumping, dancing, and playing the flute. She grows weary of his importuning and, although she agrees that he is indeed all that he claims, his antics have the effect of making her pine all the more for her Caballero. In her desperate moments she has even contemplated suicide and in this fashion is inclined to follow the example of many women of Classical literature whom she considers as paragons of virtue. The shepherd attempts to calm her feelings with his singing and playing, but all his best efforts are to no avail: "never was there greater pain./ He sings in a strange tune,/for my pain/ is greater than all others" (*Farsas*, pp. 85–86, vv. 186–89). His persistence provokes her into comments on love which suggest that the common peasant folk cannot suffer as much with it as do those from the city: "But I believe that [love] does not chastise/ those of humble lineage/ nor does it trouble them,/ so much, nor is it so fierce with them" (p. 87, vv. 267–70). This merely serves to rekindle and inflame the shepherd's own anguish and to evoke additional painful reflections from him on the subject. These are somewhat prosaic in the typically earthy style of the shepherd's language: "How my heart beats/ and how it attacks me/ since first I saw you" (p. 88, vv. 277–79), "great pain/ cold and cramps overtake me" (p. 88, vv. 287–88). When she attempts to leave, the implications are that her one solace lies in divine salvation after death, and the shepherd quickly and desperately seeks for a way out for her: he tries to distract her with the offer of tidbits he has in his hut, if she will only accompany him there, an offer, parenthetically, rather reminiscent of passages of the *Libro de buen amor* (stanzas 861–62).

But at this precise moment the Caballero appears. He has been seeking the Doncella, and immediately upon their recognition the two fly into each other's arms. As the newly-found lovers are about to depart, the shepherd begins to argue with the Caballero over the love of the damsel. The pining, love-sick role of the dainty, tremulous Doncella is now assumed by the shepherd who, now paralleling her former plaint, expresses his own querulous thoughts about the gentle passion. When the Caballero finally reveals that he has been in love with the Doncella for a long time, the shepherd, even though disconsolately, consents to the damsel's departure with her Caballero.

With the play's protagonists reconciled, in good spirits and agreeable concord, the Pastor guides the damsel and her Caballero to the road they had been seeking out of the valley. The action ends, and the play is concluded with a song by the shepherd in which he sings of the sufferings and anguish heaped upon those who are under the spell of love. This is followed by still another ballad censuring love's terrible deranging powers.

The rivalry of a shepherd and a knight for a maiden's love as presented by Fernández appeared earlier in Juan del Encina's *Égloga representada en requesta de unos amores* (1494), and this eclogue may well have served as a basis for Lucas' play. His indebtedness to it is especially evident in the parallelism of the protagonists with Encina's play. In the latter they are Pascuala, Mingo and Escudero, and these are the direct counterparts of the characters in the play by Lucas. There is, however, a deliberate, radical departure in Fernández' shepherd from Mingo. The latter can think of roses for his beloved, while the former is interested in carnal satisfaction. Therein lies an undercurrent of parody even of Encina's type of love-smitten shepherd.

Love then, and of the type that culminates in marriage, is the theme of our present play. It is typical of the humanistic, Renaissance tone and atmosphere to be found in the works of Lucas Fernández. A further aspect of the Renaissance which is manifest in this particular play is the playwright's interest in the Classics. This is best exemplified by the fact that in his play the dramatist cites Classical personages such as Queen Dido and Lucretia, in preference to biblical ones.

This play contains a character that Luis Ortiz Behety terms a favorite with Lucas Fernández, that is, a pale, disheveled damsel dressed in a coarse tunic tattered by thorns and bushes of the hillsides, who intones love's labored misfortunes in the thickets of a somber and gloomy wood.[4] The damsel is a dainty, delicate, frail, forlorn, and defenseless creature who despairs of a life without her beloved: *Quien espera, desespera;/ el que busca, anda perdido* ("He who awaits, despairs;/ he who seeks, goes about lost"), (*Farsas*, p. 83, vv. 82–83).

Yet the girl has a haughty attitude which is immediately evident when she addresses the shepherd who chances her way: "O highland shepherd,/ brother, have you seen/ a gentleman pass by?" (p. 81, vv. 16–18). She designates the shepherd as a *serrano* (highlander), but condescendingly qualifies him also as *hermano* (brother), and differentiates him immediately from her beloved *caballero* (gentleman). The maiden appears to be of gentle birth, is familiar with courtly life, and is worthy of the courtier's love for her. Lucas makes the situation somewhat more complex as he dramatizes the idea that love is as much present among the common folk as it is among the courtly gentry. The idea of love as a leveller becomes apparent in the almost presumptuous attentions the shepherd heaps upon her. Love conquers all levels of society. The maiden is amazed when the shepherd confesses love to her, "And even here love extends/ its power among shepherds?" (p. 86. vv. 208–9). When the Pastor recounts to her the suffering pangs of love among the rustics and that even the priest went around lovesick after a married woman (no doubt a satirical comment on the clergy, p. 87, vv. 235–36), the damsel admits, "I now realize/ that from east to west/ love/ subdues to his great power/ all the human people" (p. 87, vv. 262–66).

Although Lucas makes his shepherds aware that they move in a different milieu than do the men of the city, they are men who possess a strong sense of personal dignity as well. When the distressed maiden rejects his advances, the shepherd's pride is hurt and he queries: "And why not? Am I not a goodly chap?/ Well believe me that beneath the cloak/ there's really something" (p. 83, vv. 65–67). Gil Vicente later uses this same idea, namely that love is a great leveller, as a dominant theme in his *Comedia del viudo*.

This play and the *Farce of Prabos and the Soldier* begin with the same opening words: *Ay de mí, triste . . .* , ("Woe is me, sad one . . .") (p. 81, v. 1), as opposed to the *Comedy* which begins: *Dereniego del amor* ("I renounce love") (p. 59, v. 1). The

Maiden's Farce has considerable lyric quality, particularly in the
lament of the damsel: "The sweet savory springs/ will give bitter
water;/ the flowers and fresh scented roses/ will have no color
nor fragrance;/ and as a symbol of my great mourning/ the
green thickets and meadows/ will have withered their freshness"
(p. 90, vv. 361–69). The lines enunciated by the lovelorn rustic
are delightful, too, as he describes in vivid words how he suffers
the pangs of love in the deepest recesses of his heart. There is a
splendid scene in which the shepherd declares his sensuous love
for the damsel that constitutes an artful burlesque of the absurd
manner of courtly love that had been in vogue earlier. The shepherd, devoid of artificial pretenses, knows only the straightforward earth-born forms of carnal love: *de cachondiez me muero*
("I'm dying of rut") (p. 85, v. 153), and his basic approach to it
profoundly mocks the entire concept of Platonic love—obviously
one of the author's clear objectives in this as well as in the other
secular plays.

In this farce of the damsel and the gentleman, there are only
three characters to move the story along. The shepherd falls in
love with the sensual graces of the girl as he sees her approach.
But she is not interested in his attentions and instead is determined to demonstrate her free will in her love as it is embodied
in the person of her lost beloved, the courtier. The ensuing conflict centers in her attempts to subdue and reject the shepherd's
fumbling advances to her. The plot continues with her faithful
endeavors to rescue the honor of her courtier which the shepherd
jealously attacks. Presaging the strong female character appearing later in the drama of the Golden Age, as in Lope de Vega's
Fuenteovejuna, the damsel stands her ground well against the repeated entreaties and carnal motives of the shepherd. Finally,
confronted by the stubborn superiority and fanatical determina-
tion of the woman, the rustic begins to succumb to the realization
that he must give her up as a lost cause. When the courtier appears, he also tries to dissuade Pastor from loving the damsel,
and in fact reprimands him; this encounter then turns into a
veritable debate between the ordinary, coarse man and the pol-
ished courtier. The shepherd resourcefully cries out in his own
defense and actually comes to blows with the gentleman, which
results in the latter's thrashing the poor shepherd. This constitutes the major portion of the farcical element of the play. Yet the

rustic persists stubbornly in claiming the damsel, and to the courtier's warning: *no deues de curar/ de aquesta noble donzella,*
he retorts, *Muero en vella* ("you ought not to care/ about this
noble lady."/ —"I die at seeing her"), (p. 93, vv. 483–85). He
finally accepts defeat when the courtier reveals that he has loved
the woman long before the shepherd saw her. The shepherd then,
approving of their love, leads them to a new life out of the valley
of shadows and of dark despondency. Although there is no explicit indication of marriage in this play, it is strongly implied by
the couple's happy exit, and the Caballero's revealing confession
to the shepherd that he has long been in love with the girl and
that he has suffered much in his longing to possess her. The concluding *villancico* stresses the levelling theme of love: *También
nos da mal sosiego/ acá a los tristes pastores/ como en villa a
los senores* [sic] ("It also gives us a bad time/ here to us sad
shepherds/ as in town to the gentlemen"), (p. 94, vv. 545–47).

The shepherd's change of heart seems to be implausibly rapid,
unless one assumes the rustic's quick recognition of the gentleman's superiority. Obviously, such sudden changes of mind and
emotion as we saw also in the *Comedy* would be considered defects in a play dealing with a subject in a wholly serious manner;
but they can be accepted as part of the things to be taken for
granted and excused in a comedy, in which the incongruous is
standard, and this is especially true in a farcical situation. After
all, in a limited one-act play not much development of character
can really be effected, since due to exigencies of space and time,
turns of events must be somewhat brusque and therefore are to
be accepted as more or less conventional.

The author further displays an ambivalent attitude toward his
rustic characters. He highlights their speech and crudities for
the delectation of his audience which in the palace, as well as
in the church, was rather general in social structure, for it included the aristocrats as well as their servants and the common
working folk. But at the same time, the author also treats the
rustics sympathetically. They are not evil elements of society,
nor such that they should be cast away. Rather, the shepherds,
despite their crude ways and their poor formal schooling, are a
group of complex, human individuals with basically the same feelings of love, hate, and common sense as are found in the more
elevated and sophisticated courtly figures.

LUCAS FERNÁNDEZ

A suggestion of the unsettled times of which our dramatist was a product is apparent in this play. As we have noted earlier, Fernández was an ambivalent writer, combining the last throes of the relatively stagnant Medieval ideology with the refreshing humanistic spirit of the probing, exciting Renaissance. There is even an inkling of the schizophrenic ideology of the proverbial Medieval theme of the "nasty" devil in conflict with the "sweet" angel struggling simultaneously within the same person. The shepherd first assumes the role of the devil's advocate, the demon on the verge of seducing the comely maiden; then, in a turnabout that suggests a miraculous intervention of the Faith, he becomes the disenchanted, detached, magnanimous cherub who confidently guides mortals to a brighter, more rewarding life. His altruistic conduct also serves as his satisfying reward—the recompense for a good deed. Good beginnings are portended for the impending marriage. We can presume it will be a happy one, since it is based on the mutual love and trust arrived at through the exercise of independent free will capable of being tried and tested by unmerciful and harsh circumstances.

Although the author designates this play as a farce or quasi-comedy, he also refers to it simply as an "act." In his comment on the play's concluding *villancico*, he states that the song is *del mismo acto* (of the same act), (*Farsas*, p. 96). He recognized his plays, then, as performances consisting of single acts. His use of the term *auto* in the titles of two other plays is only a popular form of the more learned *acto*, which reinforces the concept of his own plays as acts.

We may conclude the appraisal of this play by quoting Angel Valbuena Prat. The renowned Spanish critic considers Fernández' work superior to Encina's corresponding eclogue "in concentration of sentiments, in sharpening of the profiles of the three characters, in precise phrases, in pure and appropriate vocabulary." [5]

III Diálogo para cantar (Dialogue for Singing), *1496–1497*

The second work in the volume of the princeps edition is the *Dialogue for Singing*, a song-drama of courtly love in a pastoral setting. The fact that the piece is bound between plays which are dated within the years 1496 and 1497 would tend to suggest that the musical act was composed in this time span. Whether or not the *Dialogue for Singing* is meant to apply to some events in the life of the ill-fated son of the Catholic Kings, the heir apparent, Prince John, who died at the age of nineteen in Salamanca, is at this time left to speculation. The thought of this possible connection is nonetheless an intriguing one.[6] Certainly, it is not out of the realm of possibility that the *Dialogue for Singing* was presented with direct reference to the prince, keeping in mind that the name of the *Dialogue*'s protagonist is Juan. It may even have been performed in his very presence while he was perhaps awaiting news of the departure for Spain of his betrothed, Margaret of Austria, daughter of Emperor Maximilian. Subsequently the Prince and his father traveled to northern Spain where they greeted the bride-to-be and escorted her to Castile. Their marriage in early 1497 in Burgos was to be of very short duration. One of the chroniclers writes: ". . . in 1497, the very year of his marriage, prince don Juan was dying, the one married to the exuberant German, Margaret, and the noble and tender prince was dying due to amorous excesses, far too many for his tender youth; so that this will serve as a precedent in future marriages of princes in order that such a disastrous end will be avoided, for this constituted a veritable misfortune. Because with don Juan, the male line of the Catholic Kings was terminated."[7] Under these circumstances Fernández' musical piece would be dated at some time in late 1496 or early 1497, before the impending marriage and the Prince's closely following death. The Prince was apparently very fond of the unrequited type of love theme and entertainment as exemplified by Fernández' *Dialogue*. Juan del Encina, for example, is known to have presented one of his eclogues of similar subject matter before the Prince in 1497. It was called *Representación del amor*. In it Cupid, with one of his darts, mortally wounds a shepherd while the latter is out hunting.[8]

This song-drama based on the traditional structure of the dialogue-song is written in twenty-two strophes of seven lines each, with eight syllables to a line with the rhyme *abbaacc*. A three-line *estribillo* (refrain) is taken from a popular song, *¿Quién te hizo, Juan, pastor/ sin gasajo y sin plazer?/ Que alegre solías ser* ("Who made you, Juan, a shepherd/ without joy and pleasure?/ For you used to be happy"), (*Farsas*, p. 77, vv. 1–3).[9] The three lines of the refrain indicate both the theme and (when the song was still being sung popularly) the basic melodic tune as well, to which the entire song-drama is written. The three-line refrain heads the *Dialogue* and is to be repeated after each seven-line strophe. Thus each stanza is extended to ten lines, with the additional lines of the refrain adding the rhyme *dcc*. Lines six and seven of each stanza end in a rhyme in -*er,* thus connecting them to the following refrain's last two lines which also rhyme in -*er.*

The song-drama under consideration is a tale that concerns Juan, a lively, life-of-the-party type of shepherd whose life abruptly changes from joy to sadness and suffering. So drastic is the change in him that it makes him almost unrecognizable to those who have known him before. This physical and mental permutation has evidently taken place due to the loss of a beloved. The loss is based on his realization that his own love has been spurned by the love object. Abandoned, he retreats into the turbulent prison of his strained sensibilities. He sadly laments his loss of strength and utters the constant belief that his illness is incurable. He has been converted into a living ghost. His friend, Bras, encourages him to overcome the conviction of his imminent demise, but Juan harbors no hope of consolation. He emphasizes the hopelessness of his malady, and identifies it as the outcome of unrequited love. He recounts his burning, intense suffering, an affliction which has become so physical that he does not have the strength to stand upright.

When Juan is exhorted to reveal the name of the beloved who cruelly spurns him and causes this enormous anguish, he at first hesitates, but later decides to acquiesce. At this point the story comes to a sudden end, and the *Dialogue for Singing* does not indicate or even imply the desired conclusion. In this confrontation between Juan and Bras, Lucas Fernández adds to the strains of unrequited love a touch of human interest, a sense of conflict and, therefore, of drama, albeit primarily of a psychological nature, as Bras attempts to get at the root of the story: at the same time that Bras fails to learn the answer he seeks, the spectators are likewise left in suspense by the author. The final stanza, which is in effect a prelude to the revelation of the name of the beloved, is not, as we have seen, followed by this revelation. We may suppose that the varying circumstances under which the dramatic song might have been sung would have provided the final stanza which would have disclosed the identity of the beloved, or it may have been subtly deduced by the spectators themselves—if we refer back to the suggestion that the *Dialogue for Singing* may have treated of Prince Juan and his love for Margaret.

Although Fernández' song-drama is not a continuous vituperation against love, in which one character adds to the comments of the other, we see here that Lucas Fernández does not present a love that is pleasant, a love of melancholy joy that most poets make of it, but rather he presents a love which is a physically destroying force, one which would have better been left unexperienced. This version of love is in effect a truly conventional one, in the courtly manner, and goes back as far as the Classical literature of ancient Greece and Rome (e.g. Plutarch's *Lives*) as well as of India (e.g. *Kama Sutra*). Fernández' dialogue thus reflects a diatribe against love's emotion, but is only slightly reminiscent of Rodrigo de Cota's *Diálogo entre el amor y un viejo (Dialogue between Love and the Old Man)*, ca. 1470.

Juan of the *Dialogue for Singing* has seen himself transformed from a strong lad adorned with ribbons into an emaciated forlorn wretch. The poetic verses are simple, yet full of expressive and pathetic force, as the shepherd, Juan, describes his state of physical languor: "And sparks never cease/ to fall in my innermost parts . . . / My bones and legbones/ shatter into a thousand pieces/ and my arms fall/ and my ribs ache" (pp. 78–79, vv. 60–61, 109–12). He is bewildered, "for love gives me great pain/ with its powers and strength,/ and I know not what to do with myself" (p. 79, vv. 93–95).

A spirit of sincere intimacy bursts forth in the shepherd's candid revelation of his love-sickness. While his companion yearns to know the reason for his suffering, Juan clings to the notion that only his eyes know the sufferings of his soul, and he will not reveal the source of his agony. Since Juan does not divulge the name of his beloved, it appears as if the *Dialogue* were incomplete and lacked a strophe. Nonetheless, from an artistic point of view, the poem ends skillfully and effectively. Moreover, the refrain in the form of a query lends a certain enigmatic melancholy to the musical piece.

F. Asenjo Barbieri and Manuel Cañete imply that what Lucas wrote in this song-drama is intended to be universal and that it contains a composite reference both to Encina and Prince Juan and to all other individuals with the same name, or with any other name for that matter. Love is after all a universally felt emotion, and its reactions are basically the same in the entire gamut between the high prince and the lowly shepherd. Even so, granting all these possibilities, we believe, as we pointed out earlier (p. 101), that the play seems to apply most to the son of the Catholic Kings. It seems to show a real-life inspiration from the royal family source. Further, it contains a clear reflection of the adventurous thinking of the day, with its ideas of conquests, victories, and glory: "you show yourself the greater conqueror,/ while greater is the evil,/ the greater is the victory over it,/ for gaining the greater glory" (p. 78, vv. 35–38). The foregoing could be interpreted as a reference to the future political promise of the young prince in whom the entire Spanish nation confidently focused its hope.[10]

The entire *Dialogue for Singing* can be read in a few minutes. But to sing one of the stanzas alone, the time needed is from seventy to ninety seconds. The twenty-two stanzas, if they were sung without pause, would last some twenty-five to thirty-five minutes. But more likely, according to the custom of the time, some musical instruments would play between the stanzas a musical sequence of the same melody. With these interludes between the stanzas, the duration of the *Dialogue for Singing* would be increased to forty or fifty minutes. So much singing in the song-drama may be a surprise, but it gives an idea of the taste for sung repartee in the opening days of the Renaissance. Even one *villancico* could take as many as ten minutes to be sung, which would be the approximate length of a popular song of the era. It is likely that the musical interludes would last about as long as the dialogue portions of a play by Fernández. This is particularly true of those his plays where we find a *villancico* in their midst, plus one or two more at the conlusion of the plays.

These *villancicos*, besides being sung, were also danced to. If we take Lucas' first *Comedy* as an example, we find a play of 565 lines of dialogue and sixty-six lines of song (including the repeated refrain after each stanza of the *villancico*). The ten percent or so of lines from the entire play destined for musical treatment would stretch out considerably in the actual presentation. The case for symmetrical balance between the musical portions and those of dialogue is even more striking with the second play, the *Maiden's Farce*, which has 523 spoken lines and 150 sung ones (when account is made again of the repeated refrain after each stanza). We can estimate the time spent in singing and dancing these and similar tunes through the musical notations retained in the *Cancionero* by Francisco Asenjo Barbieri, which also contains songs by Encina. Furthermore, the spoken and musical portions that appear to be in balance are well exemplified in Encina's *Égloga VIII* (of Mingo and Pascuala) which begins *¡Ha, Mingo, quedaste atrás!* ("Hey, Mingo, you're falling behind!"), in which there are about 485 lines of dialogue and one hundred lines for the songs. If we take into consideration the interludes by instruments between the sung verses and also the time consumed in dancing to the tunes, a portion of time equal to that consumed by the dialogue is thus easily calculated.[11] It would appear from the number of songs and dances occurring in the plays of Lucas Fernández and of Juan del Encina that a genre akin to the musical comedy is under consideration here, rather than a straightforward spoken dramatic representation. This is of course not meant to imply that straight dramatic pieces did not have a separate existence in the repertoire of the general theater in vogue at that time.

From Lucas' practice it can be surmised that he used music very effectively to augment the emotional participation of the audience in the action suggested by his dramas. It adds a gay and at times a boisterous revelry to the happy events, while in the authentically tragic *Passion Play* the music is used to express the grief and pain more effectively than mere words could have done. This is particularly true of the lament sung by the three Marys. The impact of the lyrical intensity of the words combined with music is heightened to a degree of emotion that acquires tragic dimensions.

One is inclined to agree with Charlotte Stern's penetrating, if perhaps a bit oversimplifying, comment that "It would appear . . . that the earliest literary drama grew out of the lyric and the dance, and boasted an array of musical effects that tended to eclipse the dramatic action or at least to relegate it to a decidedly inferior position." [12] The vernacular drama in Spain, though in our opinion not a direct outgrowth of the lyric and the dance, nor of the religious tropes, did certainly utilize these and related forms by incorporating some of their features, in whole or in part, into its diverse techniques, whether they were classically or popularly inspired.

CHAPTER 8

The Sacred Mystery Play,
Auto de la Pasión (The Passion Play,)
1500-1503

THE theme of the *Passion Play* enjoyed great popularity throughout the medieval period, both during the era's full bloom and its subsequent decline.[1] The passion theme, employed to commemorate the Easter celebrations, is one of those most often treated by medieval poets.

Lucas Fernández' treatment of the theme produces his most poetic and profound effort among his plays, one which is the most widely esteemed of his works. It is this composition that has earned for him the title of the "Calderón of the early theater." It has gone through at least five editions and in recent times has been recited in part or played in whole on various occasions.[2] It is not merely a play that gives aesthetic pleasure to the spectators, but is also one which inspires the believer and stimulates him to immediate devotion. It is, in effect, a mystery play which was intended as a rousing propaganda piece for the Faith. The work is packed with emotion, with grief, tears, and blood. The tragic events of the Crucifixion are recalled in graphic narration and with a deep religious intensity. The play's unique success depends to a large extent, then, not on the contemplation of primary action, but on a vigorous and dynamic narration, recited in vivid, impassioned tones by St. Peter and St. Matthew. Their exposition follows the story of St. Matthew (xxvii) and St. Luke (xxiii). Neither Christ nor the Virgin Mary takes part in the stage action (as opposed to the practice of the French mystery plays). Fernández' play thus assumes the character of a sort of theatrical elegy. In the closing scenes, it is the three Marys who give the narration a dramatic cohesiveness as we see them in their anguished, uncertain movements in search of the buried Christ, whose body they cannot discover in the tomb. The play culminates in the pacifying epilogue of the *villancico* which lends a dignified dramatic intensity to the death of Christ.

The play is based on the true biblical gospels without apochryphal embellishments or doubtful episodes. It is simply an energetic, almost an angry and anguished expression of Christ's Passion. It is presented with dignity of style and a deep and great poetic instinct.

The sequence of events is the following: Peter recites the prologue in which he mournfully laments having denied the crucified Christ three times. As he entreats forgiveness, he is met by Dionysius of Athens. The latter, a convert of St. Paul, is placed by Fernández in the time of Christ through an anachronism, a device which is frequent in the plays of the period. Peter continues to sing praises of Christ and with unrestrained emotion recalls His prayer in the garden "this" evening. (The demonstrative adjective is a clue to the possible day of presentation of the piece—Maundy Thursday.) As Peter goes on to recount Christ's betrayal by Judas and His subsequent suffering at the hands of the mob, Matthew suddenly joins in the narration and poignantly describes Christ's woeful agony. The three Marys then enter upon the scene and, after singing a dirge, join in the lamentation. At this point an *Ecce homo* is shown, moving the players to sing a song suggested by it. Now it is Matthew, rather than Peter, who further describes the scene of touching pathos of the Passion of Christ, particularly the moving scene of the weeping Mother, the *planctus Mariae* (Mary's weeping), over the lifeless body of her Son.

When Matthew recalls the Crucifixion, a cross is brought out and the actors kneel in adoration, singing a polyphonic melody that probobly has organ accompaniment. At this point the prophet Jeremiah anachronistically joins in the lamentation over Christ's death and repeats his prediction of the downfall and destruction of Jerusalem. He is the wailer of the ages, a moral and allegorical figure. He waves a flag with five blemishes to represent the five wounds of Christ. Matthew then recounts the words of the Mother Mary in the traditional Latin of the *planctus Mariae* as she moans over the body descended from the Cross. The intensity of the tragic emotion of the scene where wrongdoing frustrates the hopes of the righteous, heightened by the poetic narration, prompts a call to general adoration as Dionysius expresses his earnest desire to see Christ, since he (and the public viewing the play) had no opportunity to see Him in life. Dionysius is told that Christ has long been buried, but as a consolation he may see His "monument," the tabernacle which contains the Sacred Host. Mary Magdalene leads him to the "sepulchre" and everyone present is exhorted to worship at it. As the actors kneel, they break into song and are accompanied by organ music. The song narrates various episodes of the Lord's life, in which a remembrance of Christ's birth is linked to the tragedy of Calvary. The song thus continues the dignified dramatic intensity of the entire work, and ends on a very potent note which could, and probably did, serve as the culminating point at which the congregation partook of the Holy Communion.

The ending reminds one somewhat of revival meetings where members of the audience, after an inciting, fiery sermon, rush in a frenzy to accept the faith being offered for the salvation of their souls.

The anachronistic introduction of Sts. Dionysius and Jeremiah causes no surprise. Christ is the agonist in the play while Dionysius is the authentic protagonist.[3] His figure stands out as he exclaims, *Yo soy el más desastrado* ("I am the most unfortunate one"), (*Farsas*, p. 165, v. 317). He publicly grieves more than the others and is urgently interested in knowing the details of the Passion. He is the focal point of the dialogue as he interrupts and interrogates other characters. He thus provokes the didacticism of the religious mystery which explains the significance of the Passion. St. Dionysius' impatient desire to see Jesus even in death permits the dramatist to bring the work to a conclusion wherein he has the actors fall on their knees in adoration of the Sacred Host, a prelude to the church audience's partaking of the Holy Communion.

We find in the play a mixture of languages since St. Matthew speaks both in Latin and Spanish. Latin is adhered to particularly in the passage which quotes the words of the Mother, in the traditional manner of the *planctus Mariae*. The play was probably written before 1503, possibly as early as 1500. It seems natural to suppose that it was presented with some of the clerics and choirboys playing the various roles, and perhaps the younger ones among them performing the roles of the three Marys (if women themselves did not actually take part in the play). Dresses and shepherds' clothes were the only wardrobes that some players' groups carried with them in the sixteenth century. Such items constituted the actors' normal stage apparel. In our discussion of the Corpus Christi festivities, we did notice, however, that women appeared in the various pageants, particularly as dancers, but possibly also as actresses.

The stage area of the play is to some extent physically expandable since the actors have to move a little to go to the "sepulchre." As regards the play's intended place of presentation, we may surmise from the fact that since an *Ecce homo*, a cross, and Sacred Host are used prominently in the action, it probably took place in a church where it formed part of the Easter celebration. The expandable stage area could probably consist merely of different portions of the church. It is presumed that the Cathedral of Salamanca hosted at least some of the play's performances.

It is not clear exactly what kind of staging was used for the performances of Lucas Fernández' plays in Salamanca. Performances in different parts of the country presumably varied with the resources, ability, and taste of the director. Some productions probably took place before the very altar of the church, others to its side, or the pulpit; some would be acted out on platforms, others without them, and with or without musical accompaniment. The staging no doubt depended primarily on the resources of the producer and the funds made available to him by the people or churches that hired him. There could have been elaborate staging of multiple sets on the one hand, while on the other, mere costuming would have to suffice, with the action played out on a bare floor of a church or of the streets or courtyards where a performance could be viewed by an audience.[4]

With the help of Lucas Fernández' introductory commentary to his plays and his stage directions, together with the Salamancan Cathedral Chapter's expense accounts, we know that certain types of costumes were used by actors to represent shepherds. These costumes would include robes, shoes, cloths, and materials, such as artificial beards, wigs, and skins. We also know from the church records that organs would be carried on platforms to various parts of the city to provide the necessary musical accompaniments. Reeds and rushes were brought in for decorating the church or streets and possibly to simulate a country scene on a stage setting, but no description is provided of the very stage itself by Lucas Fernández. There is no indication of whether it was elaborate or simple, and whether it varied for his different plays. Variety of settings would probably be the general rule.

We do know that sophisticated staging was available and in use in different parts of Spain. However, very rudimentary, plain types of productions were also common.[5]

The *Passion Play* represents the culmination of the author's dramatic efforts and prepares the way for the *auto sacramental* of Spain's Golden Age. All the characters in the *Passion Play* attain heights of grandeur; they become more godlike, as befits man in his tragic state, as opposed to his more bestial self in comic episodes. This work is an early masterpiece of the Spanish stage and exemplifies its author's poetic, dramatic, and lyric acumen. It is a mature and significant work. In this Easter play Lucas shows himself superior to Encina by the work's content, development, and the poetic style which saturates it with memories of the Evangelists and the Prophets.[6] When Fernández composed this play, he was truly at home in his milieu. The warmth of his descriptions and narrations is outstanding as the play's events grow in pathos and intensity of emotion.

As the study of "The *Planctus Mariae* and the Passion Plays," by Sandro Sticca reveals, the Crucifixion is a venerated and common theme.[7] In Spanish literature we need not seek further for it than in the *Libro de buen amor,* in which Juan Ruiz speaks *De la Pasión de Nuestro Señor Jesuxristo* (strophes 1059–66). The play had its antecedents in Spain and also in the mystery and miracle plays of the French, Italian, and English medieval periods.[8] The theatricalization of this pious theme by Lucas Fernández was written to stimulate and kindle the devotion of those witnessing the performance, since it elucidates the victorious conception of life over death as a part of the ideology of medieval asceticism. The audience is encouraged to feel pity for God, the Son, as St. Peter intones: "Let us cry aloud and in shouts/ since our sovereign God/ and human/ is exposed to such affliction" (*Farsas,* p. 159, vv. 97–100). The didactic purpose is further made clear by Peter's repeated calls to the spectators for attention as he entreats from the very start of the act: "Hear my grieved voice,/ hear, ye loving of the world,/ hear the raging passion,/ which in His precious humanity/ our God is suffering" (p. 157, vv. 1–5).

The play, despite, or perhaps because of, its didactic overtones, is becoming popular again today after four and a half centuries. It is presented by school and religious groups as well as by professionals, or read and recited before the general public in evening poetry readings at such esteemed places as the Ateneo of Madrid. On one evening the present writer had occasion to hear poems read and recited by the actor José Ramón Centenero in a program which included portions from the works of Lope de Vega, Calderón de la Barca, José Zorrilla, Antonio Machado, Juan Ramón Jiménez, and García Lorca. It began with a recitation from the Easter play by Lucas Fernández. In his interpretation of some poignantly dramatic excerpts of the play, Centenero was very emotional, actually creating a sensation of anger rather than one of compassion. Following the dictum of the initial invocation by St. Peter, the actor shouted his lines with feverish fury. He concluded the recitation with his arms extended and his voice raging with anger. When his arms fell to his sides, there was a pause which was then spontaneously broken with thunderous applause from the audience.

The lines recreated in this fashion by the actor were those of St. Matthew, beginning: *O, qué fue verle acusar* ("Oh, what it was to see Him accused"), (p. 165, v. 342), and ending with: *Dad, Señora, dad mandado/, en la corte celestial/ que tienen su Rey cercado/ y maltratado/ por la culpa paternal* ("Lady, give the order/ in the celestial court,/ for they have their King besieged/ and maltreated/ for the paternal guilt"), (p. 168, vv. 452–56). Such lines, when interperted properly, can indeed arouse the Spanish soul.

In his beautiful discussion of this play, Alfredo Hermenegildo isolates three progressive visual stages that lead the spectators to identify themselves as participants in the confession of the Faith and adoration of Christ: [9] (1) after St. Peter recounts his grief, St. Dionysius and Mary Magdalene offer a release of cathartic emotion by encouraging the audience to give vent to its feelings through tears: ("Let us all cry; let us cry/ let us cry a bitter cry"), (p. 165, vv. 312–13). Lucas then used the expedient of the *Ecce homo,* a scene of the suffering Christ crowned with thorns; this inspires the spectators to devotion. The actors show their veneration by kneeling and bursting into a song: *Ecce homo, Ecce homo,* etc.; (2) The devotional submission to the Faith is emphasized when, just as abruptly as the *Ecce homo,* the Cross is made to appear at the instant when Mary Magdalene narrates the tragedy of Holy Friday. Once again the players fall to their knees and sing the "Hymn of the Cross," which even today is chanted in the liturgical acts while the individuals kneel; (3) finally, this shock-effect is brought to a climactic crescendo of devotion when the "tomb" of Christ is displayed for contemplation. The actors once more fall on their knees before the representation of the Lord's "grave" as they sing the closing hymn of the *Passion Play* and the spectators join in the religious adoration. Through participation, the parishioners identify quickly with the religious ritual, and experience the stimulating fervor that is one of the chief objectives of the play's performance.

The temporal and spatial realism is thrown to the winds with the anachronistic introduction of Sts. Dionysius and Jeremiah.[10] Dionysius is converted to the Faith and becomes most bitter in his condemnation of the treason by Judas. In his medieval intolerant attitude toward other religions, Lucas considered the whole Jewish nation as an evil element in diabolical association with Judas in the betrayal and crucifixion of Christ. In comparison, Gil Vicente was much more tolerant on this point, as he reveals in his letter to John III of Portugal in 1531, in which he defends the Jews as a redeemable people. Portugal, in general, had a more benevolent, humane, and enlightened attitude toward Judaism; and, by the time Vicente wrote the letter, the humanistic, tolerant thinking had taken a firmer hold on the intellectuals.

There may be something to the idea proposed by Alfredo Hermenegildo, in his study mentioned above, that the *Passion Play* comes at a significant juncture in Lucas' life, that is, at a time when he decides to become a cleric. His Renaissance attitudes demonstrated in the profane and semireligious plays revert to a more medieval, fervently religious orientation in this play. He comes to grips with what he seems to consider "true" religion. In a sense, "he has seen the light," and thus approaches a more ascetic outlook on the essence of life.

Interestingly, Hermenegildo identifies Dionysius with Lucas Fernández: a wise man who, when unable to cope with questions of nature, turns to Christ for his consolation. Hermenegildo sees Lucas' personal involvement with Christ when Lucas espouses the clerical profession, represented in his play by Dionysius' conversion. Dionysius is therefore Lucas' alter ego. Behind the robes of Dionysius, Lucas dramatizes his own spiritual experience: "Let's go, brothers, to see him/ since I did not see him in life" (p. 175, vv. 736–37). The implication here would be that Lucas in his Renaissance worldly ways did not know Christ and was therefore unhappy until he found Him. This is an interesting insight into the dramatist's life made by Hermenegildo, who is the first to make an attempt at identifying any one character of Fernández' plays with the dramatist himself. Hermenegildo sees the change of the worldly figure of Lucas Fernández turning spiritually more puritanic with his advancing adult years.

In an earlier section we have made some allusion to the role of women in Lucas' plays. In the *Passion Play* we are led to see a different aspect of the woman's personality. She is no longer the playful lass of the secular plays, but rather she becomes a tragic, innocent creature victimized by circumstances from which she cannot extricate herself. She must stoically endure the sorrows that are set upon her frail shoulders. But though her body is weak, her ability to endure sufferings of unimaginable proportions makes her stand out almost as a divine personality. We are presented with a woman who is imbued with strong maternal instincts. She will bear all her adversities with headstrong faith, with a deeply-felt resignation to the unchangeable events—events that are not susceptible to modification even when she exerts her strongest efforts. Resignation to life through faith is the most admirable quality in this picture of the woman of Lucas Fernández' last play.

The Easter play describes the circumstances and emotions immediately following the descent from the Cross. We are told how the delicate, sensitive woman, the Virgin Mother, places her Son's head on her lap, bringing to the scene a note of deep human pathos: *Con sus lágrimas lauaua/ las llagas y las heridas;/ con su velo las limpiaua/ y enxugaua,/ con angustias doloridas* ("With her tears she washed/ the sores and the wounds;/ she cleaned them with her veil,/ and wiped them/ with painful afflictions"), (p. 173, vv. 641–45). The three Marys seeing the descent, Mary Salome, Mary Magdalene and Mary Cleophas, are equally tormented by the death of the Redeemer. Indeed, the three Marys seem to register no distinct individualities. Even their words are headed at times in the play's princeps edition simply by M. so that one does not know which of the three is speaking. As they speak of the most tender moments of the descent from the Cross, they speak as though all three were a single woman: "How disconsolate we went/ wretched among the wretched/ when we wanted to remove/ the crown, we could not/ pull out the thorns" (p. 175, vv. 726–30).

The language of the piece is natural and smooth-flowing, with very few regional traits, while there are a goodly number of passages in Latin, when the characters address the Diety. Indeed, it seems that for Lucas Fernández and his audience, God spoke only in Latin. The three Marys and the saints are also somewhat more than human; they are actually considered almost to be divine, and consequently their speech is portrayed slightly out of the ordinary both in tone and in a lexical shift. There is evidence of a mystical use of language in the reference to Christ's sacrifice which is metaphorically compared to the pelican's. The pelican was believed to have fed its fledgelings by tearing apart its breast and letting them devour its flesh. The play's potent funereal lyricism paints a picture of the agonizing, grotesque image of Christ seen so frequently in Spanish churches, where it provides the people with a stark reminder of their Faith: *Mirá este cuerpo sagrado/ como está lleno de plagas;/ muy herido y desgarrado;/ toda está descoyuntado* ("Look at this sacred body/ how covered it is with sores,/ most wounded and torn;/ all of it is rent asunder") (p. 174, vv. 706–9).

Nowhere is the power of Fernández' language so deeply felt as in this Easter play on Christ's Passion. The poetry is easy-flowing and filled with elevated concepts. The author makes the *Passion Play* one of his most memorable, vivid, and moving incidents taken from the *New Testament*. It is a piece that harbors a most beautiful lyric inspiration. The vigor of dramatic narration is at its best in this work by the Salamancan author. The poet has the difficult task of presenting a dramatic piece without the intervention of primary action. The interest in it is therefore awakened not by the action, but by means of a vigorous and energetic poetry which is full of human tension and dynamism. Yet through it all, the language is uncomplicated, direct, and simple. We find, even so, several instances of antithesis as in *¡O, quán dulce es el llorar/ . . . y quán dulce lamentar,/ y quán dulces los gemidos!* ("Oh, how sweet it is to cry/ . . . and how sweet to lament,/ and how sweet the moans!"), (p. 165, vv. 337–41).

The repetition of terms in other instances has the effect of deepening the mysterious enigmas of religious faith: *O, mengua de mi gran mengua* ("Oh, disgrace of my great disgrace"), (p. 158, v. 40); *O, principio principal;/ o, causa prima y primera* ("Oh, principal beginning;/ oh, first and foremost cause"), (p. 160, vv. 136–37). The auditory effect of such repetition, of course, is unfortunately lost in the translation.

The *Passion Play* has a surprising paucity of verbs and adjectives. Nonetheless, it has its own dynamic movement because their absence is mitigated by the past and present participles which function as adjectives and verbs. The participle becomes a synthesizing element by which the author reduces the number of words and integrates the two functions into one. Such compression brings a dramatic intensity to the narration. This effect can be seen clearly in the following lines: *O, qué fue verle acezando/ con vna cruz muy pesada,/ cayendo y estropeçando,/ y leuantando,/ con la cara ensangrentada;/ con la boz enrronquecida,/ rompidas todas las venas,/ y la lengua enmudecida,/ con la color denegrida,/ cargado todo de penas* ("Oh, what it was to see Him gasping/ with a very heavy Cross,/ falling and stumbling,/ and rising,/ with a bloodied face;/ all veins broken,/ and His tongue silenced,/ with a blackish color,/ all weighted with pains"), (p. 167, vv. 392–401).

The participial adjectives designate violent emotions and concurrently enliven the images by means of descriptions perceptible to the eyes, ears, and touch—in a word, the delicate sensory organs are bombarded to arouse compassion for almost unbearable physical pain. The abundance of adjectives thus counteracts the lack of verbs.

Lucas Fernández enhances his dynamic narrations further by the use of active verbs which often pertain to violence, and, as might be expected, there is a scarcity of the verbs "to be," *ser* and *estar*. This is in consonance with the grief of the actors and the corporal pain of Christ himself: *llorar* (to cry), *gemir* (to moan), *repelar* (to pull out hair), *llagar* (to wound), *arrancar* (to pull out), etc. Even the past participles as adjectives infuse dynamism into the work through their implicit verbal function: *encendido* (inflamed), *desastrado* (unfortunate), *lastimado* (hurt), *ensangrentado* (bloodied), *atenazado* (clenched), etc.

Alongside these verbs is the predominance of the infinitive, both as an active verb and as a noun. In fact, the infinitive surpasses in number the verbal forms in the present tense by 126 to 115 in the *Passion Play*. The preponderant use of the infinitive in this narrative play amounts to twice the frequency found in the other plays of our author, even when compared to the other tenses as a group. In the play the infinitive is found in the ratio of one to four verbs, while the ratio of the infinitive to other verbal forms in the other plays is roughly one to seven. The use of the infinitive supplies an atmosphere of absolute activity which conforms with the divine religious context. The extraordinary facts referring to the death of Christ acquire greater emotive force, a more complete sensation of divinity through the infinite character of the infinitive.

The deepening effect of emotion is achieved likewise by the use of simple poetic devices. (For audience comprehension they could not be complicated; they would merely lose their effect as a result of possible incomprehension.) There is extensive use of vocalic and consonantal alliteration, and the use of derivational repetition of words as *principio principal* (principal beginning). Among the list of devices besides alliteration are parallel construction, anaphora, redoubling of words, and simple repetition of the same sound several times in one sentence: *y el beber de mi viuir* ("and the drinking of my living"), (p. 158, v. 34); *por el pecado primero* ("by the first sin"), (p. 159, v. 75); *Su sangre sancta, sagrada* ("His holy, sacred blood"), (p. 160, v. 116); *siempre, siempre predicaua* ("always, always He preached"), (p. 160, v. 134); *quando quitar le quisimos* ("when we wanted to remove") (p. 175, v. 727). In addition, the presence of internal rhyme, with its greater rhythm, augments the emotional impact of the words: *mi limpieza, mi pureza* ("my cleanliness, my purity"), (p. 158, v. 53); *miserere, pues que muere* ("miserere, since He's dying"), (p. 158, v. 58). It can be seen, then, that Lucas relies heavily upon the emotional affectiveness of empirical rhetoric, for in poetic dramas like his, enunciation, and not the action, acquires a degree of utmost importance.

The author thus employed a language suitable to the occasion and appropriate for the exposition of sacred tragedy. It is normal, standard Castilian, except for an isolated example or two of the Salamancan dialect. Lucas avoided superfluous language and instead wrote clearly and smoothly for quick comprehension. The play has been eminently successful owing to Lucas' extraordinary ability to make the narration so vibrant and of such high dramatic impact that it almost simulates the action as this would have been presented on stage itself. In this rests the true art of Fernández' *Passion Play*.

CHAPTER 9

Semireligious Plays; Nativity Plays

LUCAS' two semireligious plays deal with the revelation of the birth of the Christ Child to the shepherds. Both dramas are interwoven with scenes from daily life and with satire of certain institutions. In these plays Lucas elaborates the sacred birth with a lyrical vein, while he introduces a considerable amount of didactic material as well. He treats the topic of Christ's birth with a mixture of doubt and somber religious profundity. Though it is not a topic of greater universal import than the one of love which he utilized for his earlier plays, he tries to treat the Nativity theme with more philosophical depth. He undertakes to present an event with a long history of literary evolution behind it, even in Spain. Even though W. L. Grant asserts that the early Nativity plays of Europe owe their development to Neo-Latin religious pastoral poems,[1] one may ask whether it is necessary to assume that the Medieval Nativity play developed from a simpler form, such as the pastoral poem. These poems, according to Grant's studies, appear near the middle of the fourteenth century, but Nativity plays in the vernacular, like the *Auto de los Reyes Magos,* were extant as early as the middle part of the twelfth century. Indeed, there are records of other early performances of the manger scene. A half century after the *Auto de los Reyes Magos* there is mention in 1304 of another play dealing with the birth of Christ.[2] And, as we have seen earlier, other performances of the Nativity play as well as of other types of religious and farcical drama existed elsewhere on the European continent. The objective of the religious play was to reawaken, or to reinforce and restore, the spectators' faith in the birth of the Messiah, and to remind them of their heritage—the road to ultimate salvation and redemption on the final, last Day of Judgment.

I Égloga del nacimiento (Eclogue of the Nativity), *1500*

This piece, which hinges on the revelation of the birth of Christ to the shepherds, is one of the two semireligious plays. Its full title is *Égloga o farsa del nacimiento de Nuestro Redentor Jesucristo (Eclogue or Farce of the Birth of Our Redeemer Jesus Christ)*. The play is written in 646 lines of verse which include both the dialogue and the sung portions of the play. It appears to have been written not merely for the sake of entertainment, but also with the purpose of presenting religious dogma. Its protagonists' roles are distributed among three energetic shepherds, Bonifacio, Gil, and Marcelo, and a learned hermit, Macario.

Bonifacio begins the play with a conventional monologue in which he voices his own praises, extolling his capacity to jump, wrestle, and play music. Gil then arrives and scoffs at Bonifacio's abilities by recalling mythological figures such as Antaeus, Hercules (whose name the shepherd cannot at first recall), Narcissus, and biblical figures, Absalom, for example, who are widely known to be Bonifacio's superiors in certain ways. The reference to these figures by the rustic is perhaps a bit unusual, since he thereby exhibits a certain amount of learning. This is unexpected by Bonifacio, who considers Gil a little insane *(lloco)* anyway; but this display of education plus evidence that other shepherds like Gil, in Gil Vicente's *Auto pastoril castellano*, are also surprisingly learned, perhaps can be explained by the fact that such names kept coming up rather frequently in the literature of the day, possibly kept in the public mind from the pulpit. Especially did the names come up in the vernacular drama. The two shepherds then strive to outdo each other in boasting, not merely bragging of their physical prowess, but also of their unequalled ability to milk cows and goats, shear sheep, make traps, etc., etc., until finally, in their mania for achieving superiority, they resort to a narration of their respective lineages. Though embarrassingly humble, these ancestral lines are, amusingly for the audience, one of the shepherds' mainstays of pride and vanity. Bonifacio boasts of his grandmother, who it turns out is a veritable Celestina.

Gil is overcome with drowsiness, and Bonifacio's patience is strained to the utmost as he tries to keep his partner awake. To convince the latter of the necessity to remain awake, he cites biblical characters such as Samson, whose fate was sealed when

LUCAS FERNÁNDEZ

he fell asleep. At this point Macario, the hermit, chances upon
them. He is lost and is looking for his way back to the road which
is increasingly more difficult for him to find because night has
fallen. In a maliciously curious way, the shepherds attempt to
find out the hermit's intentions. Their indiscretions multiply and
intensify until they and Macario almost come to blows. Macario
admonishes them to stay away from him, invoking the name of
Christ, who, he confidently feels, is surely soon to come to bring
peace to the world. The shepherds' curiosity is aroused at this,
and they question Macario about the impending event. His
answer includes a naming of the biblical prophets who foretold
Christ's coming. The group is then interrupted by the sudden
entrance of Marcelo, the third shepherd, with the electrifying
news that Christ has just been born of a virgin.

The first two shepherds express doubts about the feasibility of
virgin birth. They continue to question Macario on the incarna-
tion of God and on the lineage of the Virgin. The hermit, in explanation, cites to them authoritative sources from the *Old Testament*. Marcelo claims to have seen the Holy Child and the Mother
Mary, and now overcome with joy, he wants to buy some swad-
dling clothes for the Infant. At this point Gil and Bonifacio are
finally convinced of the coming of Christ. Discord gives way to
concord, and they all plan to visit the manger and to bear gifts
to the Child. They depart singing a *villancico* which summarizes
the remarkable birth, and exhorts all to rejoice. All ills can now
be cast away since God's presence is felt on earth. Thus the insolent, doubting shepherds become faithful believers when they
comprehend the significance of the news brought to them. They
open their hearts to hope, and feel the contentment of the penetrating beatifical redemption. They radiate an unqualified trust
in the natural goodness and perfectibility of man as they go to
the stable in Bethlehem singing, and presumably dancing in their
typical country fashion.

The intervention of Macario, a learned and devout individual,
in the midst of the humble, ignorant, and skeptical shepherds
with the intended purpose of explaining the meaning of the
sacred phenomenon for all mankind, serves also a secondary purpose—that of providing an element of contrast between his correct, cultured language and the humorous, rustic dialect peculiar

[120]

to the shepherds. In addition, his august aloofness provides an elegance and a touch of sublimity to the story of the Christ Child.

In the traditional Nativity play, such as the *Representación del nacimiento de Nuestro Señor* (*ca.* 1450) by Gómez Manrique, or in the pastoral scene of the *Vita Christi* (*ca.* 1482) by Fray Iñigo de Mendoza, when the angel tells the shepherds that Christ is born, they rush off to worship Him without casting the slightest note of doubt on the holy occurrence. In Lucas Fernández we find a slight divergence from this pattern in that the attitude of the shepherds, at the initial stage at least, is one of doubting Thomases. The illiterate and the ignorant are not convinced more readily of the coming of the Christ Child than are the more learned individuals; as a matter of fact, the more informed Macario is precisely the one who is more receptive than are the shepherds to the new event. He has been prepared for it through his studies of the Prophets. The medieval ecclesiastical debates on the virginity of the Mother, as we see in this scene, however, had not been entirely eliminated nor definitively resolved by the Church.

The conspicuous anachronisms in the scenes adhere to a perfectly acceptable tradition of the period. The mention of the pope, earlier in the play, indicates that these are not the pre-Christian biblical shepherds, but rather those of the Salamancan region whose peculiar dialect they speak. Marcelo is the embodiment of both the biblical and the Salamancan types of shepherds. Through him the birth of Jesus becomes an event of the historical present. It is recreated and relived, insofar as Fernández can recapture it, with each year's successive exposure, and, in a sense, it becomes part of contemporary history; perhaps, as Fernández would have it, a symbol of the periodic rebirth of man's spirit.

The double generic classification by which the play is designated, eclogue or farce, may be explained by the fact that it combines the elements of an eclogue, a dramatic pastoral dialogue in verse, as interpreted earlier by Encina, and of the slapstick farce, as it prevails later in Lope de Rueda.

In this play, as in others by Fernández, we see several items reminiscent of the jolly elements of Juan Ruiz's *Libro de buen amor:* the shepherd's pride in his physical agility of jumping, dancing, playing the flageolet; the continued insistence of his presumed incomparable mastery of these exploits; his egotistical and naive belief in his supposed unique talents; his description of his finery, his Sunday clothes that mean so much to him, because they make him feel superior to others when he puts them on (he is always haunted by his low social status and tends to overcompensate for it); all this which appears in Fernández' play is noted in its embryonic form in portions of the earlier *Libro de buen amor* (e.g. strophes 999–1001).

The immediate popularity of the bawdy protagonist in *La Celestina* (1499) is made unmistakably clear by the mention of her name in this play by Lucas. The passage which describes Bonifacio's grandmother is a depiction of the famous go-between.[3] While the tragic lovers, Calisto and Melibea, remained relatively unknown (they are never mentioned by Lucas) even in Salamanca, which is the possible locale of their tragic lives, the fame of Celestina was undeniably notorious.

The last line of the introductory synopsis *(argumento)* of Fernández' play, written in Latin, almost as an invocation, *Et incipit feliciter sub correptione Sanctae Matris Ecclesiae* (And it begins happily under the sanction of the Holy Mother Church), discloses that the eclogue was actually corrected, approved, and therefore backed by the Church (with the meaning of "sanction" here interpreted as approbation rather than reproach), for as the records show in the course of our Chapter 4 that Lucas Fernández was hired and paid by the council of the Cathedral of Salamanca to produce similar plays, thus the Church with its hiring of Fernández and its approval of his program's contents would, in effect, patronize them. The disclosure of the church's involvement can also be here interpreted to imply that the play was ostensibly presented in the cathedral itself. We have already seen that Lucas was paid by the chapter of the Cathedral of Salamanca to present such plays as this.

One may be surprised that the Church would permit the uncouth, and at times indecent, phrases and words to be uttered by some of the rustic characters. Yet these earthy phrases were possibly even more readily accepted in those days than they would be today, even with our permissive morality. Few need be reminded that mores and manners of society change from time to time in a fairly recurrent cyclical pattern. What is viewed with shocked distaste as indecency, or perhaps as pornography in one period, is accepted as perfectly natural in other epochs. González

Pedroso observed that "even the strangest acts, and even the most remote inventions from what we today understand would please the majesty of God, could enter and comprise that universal *Sursum corda* ['lift up your hearts'—words of the Preface of the Mass] simply by sheltering themselves in the friendly shadow of a crucifix, under the vaults of a consecrated place."[4] And after all, in what other places except in a church, or in those related to or associated with the church, could a popular audience gather. The alternatives available were the public plaza or the lecture halls of the university. Only smaller and more selective groups could form in the city hall or in the private palaces. Hence the church building at times served the purpose merely of a social hall and as such, in a sense devoid of its sanctity, it readily harbored life's multifaceted manifestations.

The setting of our play is outdoors. The physical movement transpires primarily during the unraveling of the comic element, while in the remaining portions of the act, those portions which are derived from religious inspiration, the author relies somewhat more heavily on the narrative device. There are no superfluous characters in the play. Each one is necessary, and each one appears at an appropriate moment to add something vital to the work.

The theme of this play (as in the one following that we will discuss) is different from that of the preceding three secular ones, since, with the change in them from a parody of courtly love to an acceptable form of religious parody, there also comes a change in the purpose of the work. Whereas the first three works that we discussed—as recalled, they were the first three of Fernández' plays—have as their principal goal the entertainment of the public at a wedding party, this eclogue was probably presented in conjunction with a religious service at Christmas time. There is a dramatic shift in focus from the trivial troubles of the disdained lover in the plays about love to the more obvious hardships of the working, country breadwinner who is only too willing to find relief in Faith from his drudging existence.

Even at the beginning, the play irradiates a different tone from the preceding ones in that the shepherd is, for a change, happy. He is self-satisfied rather than disgusted with his fate. This disposition immediately marks the play as different from the pastoral tradition of courtly love and its mocking variants.

There remains even in this semireligious theatrical composition the aim of entertaining by means of the wiles of a comic character. The play contains a vein of rustic buffoonery that even satirizes the idiosyncracies of the very ecclesiastic potentates that encouraged these types of plays. We see a note of simple anticlerical humor as Gil directs himself with sarcasm to the hermit: *Gran famulario/ deuéys ser./ Rezáys nesse calendario,/ ¿soys bisodia, o soys almario?* ("You must be a great scholar./ You pray [with] that calendar,/ are you a phantom or a soul cupboard?"), (*Farsas,* p. 128, vv. 276–79). *Almario* is a dialectal formation combining *alma* (soul) and *armario* (cupboard) to apply jocosely to the hermit's figure.

The farce clearly had a didactic intent, characteristic of the old morality plays, which is seen in the concluding song that emphasizes the birth of Christ: "Let it be manifest to all/ that this is our eternal Lord,/ born little and tender/ of a Virgin from Galilee,/ Light of the nation of Judea,/ its Savior and Guardian" (p. 136, vv. 605–10).

The synchronic juxtaposition of two diametrically opposed attitudes toward religion seen in this play: awe and reverence, on the one hand, and parody or even blasphemy and derision on the other, is a phenomenon that neither began nor ended in medieval times, but which appears wherever religion exists. The alternation of the jocose and the serious provides an aesthetic balance for the play's structure, giving it movement, excitement, and periodic change of pace for dramatic relief. There are several ingredients that mix freely in this pastoral, religious play: the sacred Palestinian events, the rustic boorishness, and Classical mythology. There are also traces of hagiographic material in the names of San Ginés (p. 128, v. 272), and San Hilario (p. 218, v. 280). If we had information on names of religious brothers in the Salamancan cloisters, we might possibly discover that those names mentioned in the play could have been humorous references to contemporary friars in Salamanca. Fray Zorrón and Egidio are strong possibilities for such whimsical usage. Among what may seem to be allusions to topical events is a possible reference to some students who may have caused disturbances in the academic year 1498–99: "Perhaps he's the scholar/ who caused the rain and hail/ last year in our place" (p. 129, vv. 301–3). Although the pastoral, picaresque element shows up but

sporadically in Lucas Fernández' works, there are, as we have
noticed, very vivid reminders of *La Celestina* in the antiheroic
and the picaresque features of this *Eclogue of the Nativity*. The
shepherd's picaresque penchant for making fun of others is admitted by Gil when he tells Macario: "We play bigger jokes/ on
many other gentlemen./ Why do you get mad?" (p. 129, vv.
313–15). Indeed, Frida Weber de Kurlat maintains that the
simple shepherd of the sixteenth-century theater evolves into the
crafty knave of the picaresque novel.[5] It is her contention that
the antihero is the culmination of what she terms the antigeneal-
ogy which is used as a satiric recourse born in the comic nature
of the Renaissance vernacular drama. Lucas was aware of the
picaresque currents that had appeared in the medieval books of
exempla and in the tales revolving around the proverbial rogue,
Pedro de Urdemalas, whom the shepherds recollect in their confrontation with the hermit (p. 129, v. 306).

The revelations of religious dogma are made by the hermit
Macario, whose learning is such that he can even make use of
Latin. The name Macario, meaning "happy" in Greek, is significant, for he explains the tidings of great joy and happiness
brought to the shepherds by their companion, Marcelo. The explanation of the dogma was generally made in the liturgical
theater by the angel. Here it is a shepherd who makes the revelation of the birth, and it is another human, the hermit, who explains it. Thus Fernández creates a new, more human, basic
theatrical motive which gradually extends from the Nativity plays
to others of similar religious concern. The hermit further explains
the Holy Trinity which is an almost incomprehensible obstacle
to the rustics. When this hurdle is overcome, as if edified by the
Holy Spirit itself, all join in the adulation of the Virgin Mary.

The description of the Nativity is made in cultured rather than
rustic speech, but the expressive force of the language is the
same in both styles, whether rustic or elevated. This play lacks
the manger scene which is the usual climactic moment for similar
pastoral plays. Lucas prefers a discussion to a re-creation of the
sacred event, a method which he develops so well also in the
Passion Play. The players do speak of going to the manger, but
whether or not there was a manger set up near the stage to which
the shepherds went, is open to question. The manger scene was
perhaps left only to the imagination, as a concluding episode

played out in people's tradition-bent minds. The action of the play closes at a point where the shepherds discuss the gifts they prepare to take and give to the Messiah. Their Christmas gifts are not their most esteemed treasures by which their love of God could be gauged, but they are rather ordinary items of their daily lives. Their unpretentious offerings are in keeping with their practical simplicity.

The play is followed with the four characters singing in four-part harmony a carol of six stanzas, each with a Latin refrain on Christ's birth. The first stanza begins *Manifiesto a todos sea/ qu'est 'es nuestro Dios eterno* ("Let it be clear to all/ that this is our eternal God"), (p. 136, vv. 605–6). A second song, which is merely indicated by a title, *Et homo factus est* (And He was made man), we are told was sung *en canto de órgano* (in polyphonic voices), with possible organ accompaniment.[6] A dance set to these songs may have followed, thus to continue and conclude the performance.

The date of composition for this eclogue is deduced by Emilio Cotarelo y Mori to be the year 1500.[7] He infers this from the fact that the secular jubilee, or Holy Year of Rome, is vaguely alluded to by one of the shepherds who, speaking of Macario, says: "Tell me, is this friar Fox,/ the one who these days was going around/ with very holy devotion/ for the composition,/ swindling guilds?/ Is he going to get the holy pardon?"[8] Cotarelo y Mori argues that if it were not a question of a contemporary event, the Holy Year would not be recalled through the wandering of the hermit.

II Auto del nacimiento (Play of the Nativity), *1500–1502*

The full title of the play is *Auto o farsa del nacimiento de Nuestro Señor Jesucristo (Play or Farce of the Nativity of Our Lord Jesus Christ)*. Like the preceding play, this one centers around the revelation of the birth of Christ. The atmosphere of the initial scene does not give any reliable indication of what is to follow inasmuch as it begins with a shepherd's complaint of the weather, and with the introduction by him of the *carpe diem* (seize the day) theme. Yet unlike the conditions in the *Eclogue of the Nativity*, where Macario explained the difficult and controversial theological issues as well as the prophecies on the coming of the Messiah, in this work Lucas Fernández has inno-

vated further to the exent that he has expanded the role of the
shepherds to include the functions performed earlier by the
hermit. It is one of the humble shepherds who is given the responsibility of explaining the birth of Christ, including the
religious dogma that accompanies it. Thus the shepherd's usually
dull-witted actions are here forsaken and he is lifted above those
of his peers who are often portrayed as cowardly, boastful,
boisterous, and ludicrous individuals.

The play opens with Pascual describing the scene of the action
—a meadow on a cold and wet morning. The shepherd here
complains not of love as in the secular plays, but of inclement
weather. He also becomes philosophical: *En este mundo mez-*
quino/ aquel que se tiene en poco/ es semejado por lloco ("In
this wretched world/ he who thinks little of himself/ is like a
madman"), (*Farsas,* p. 140, vv. 19–21). His philosophy is to eat
and drink well and enjoy life with good company. He is hungry
and longingly thinks of things to eat. He decides to build a small
fire to warm himself and to prepare some victuals. He entertains
the idea that his food will taste better if he has company at his
side: *El prazer y el reholgar/ que no es bien comunicado/ no es*
entero gasajado ("Pleasure and amusement/ which is not well
shared/ is not complete joy"), (p. 140, vv. 46–48). He goes to
his friend, Lloreynte, whom he finds asleep, and experiences
difficulty in awakening him.

When Pascual finally succeeds in rousing Lloreynte from his
heavy sleep, they both wonder at the meaning of the great profusion of stars that covered the skies. They marvel at the sweet
singing of the birds they heard during the night, and they comment on the personal discontent they had felt at all these unusual signs. They believe someone will surely be able to explain
the meaning of these to them: "The cleric will tell us,/ and if
he doesn't, then the quack will" (p. 143, vv. 154–55), and in the
meantime they decide to play a game that will warm them up.
As they are playing and warming up to an argument, they are interrupted by Juan, who, after crossing himself in the name of
Jesus, jumps down to them from a high crag. He enthusiastically
tells them that he has heard the angel of the Lord who came to
him and announced the birth of Christ. His two friends doubt
the likelihood of what he reports, but when he recounts the
revelations of the Prophets concerning the coming of the Messiah,

they are so impressed by his learning that they give in to his arguments and determine to render homage to the Child. Pedro, a fourth shepherd, comes and he, like Juan, has seen "flying men," as he calls them. This helps to corroborate Juan's story. Then Lloreynte repeats the suggestion that they ought to go adore the Child and praise the Virgin. Each names a modest, rustic gift he will take to the Redeemer. The shepherds plan to give such rural gifts as a duck, a kid, a lamb, milk, etc. The offerings that they prepare for the Holy Child, similar to those of the preceding eclogue, are not of the type the Three Kings tender, but are much more earthy and ordinary, as befits the simple, provincial life of the shepherd. The text of the drama does not make it clear that the presents are for the Infant Jesus, but this may be taken for granted since such is the normal development of things in a Nativity play in which the shepherds' plans for a visitation tend to be the culminating point of the Christmas worship service. After the enumeration of gifts, the shepherds then decide to sing, but unable to agree on who should begin, they call Minguillo, who happens to be nearby, and he accepts their invitation to lead them. They terminate the play by dancing and singing two *villancicos* which exhort and encourage the audience to rejoice in the glory of the birth of Christ.

Although part of the ending of this play may be considered technically weak since a call is made offstage at the very last moment to summon Minguillo in order to form a quartet which is required by the theatrical convention for a musical finish, we can usually see in contrast a general tendency in Lucas' plays toward the integration of the various characters into the major part of the action.

The play is constructed in three noticeably distinct parts: (1) the humorous scene with the sleepy Lloreynte, (2) the transition and change in mood occasioned by Juan's appearance, and (3) the Epiphany and explanation by Juan and Pedro Picado of the coming of the Messiah, and that holy event's interpretation. Religious dogma and didacticism, then, underlie the third portion of the play. Discernible, also, is a gradual progression in characterization technique of the author as he depicts the frisky shepherds, first with their naive emotions, and then as he has them mature in their attitude when they comprehend the significance of the birth of Christ.

After the initial joviality of the early scenes, the shepherds put aside their irreverent jokes and become increasingly more serious, raising the social tone of their speech to the point that it becomes somewhat more elegant and learned than their humble background would seem to warrant. We have seen on an earlier occasion that Gil of the *Eclogue of the Nativity* evidenced a certain amount of mythological and biblical knowledge. This may in part be a reflection of the concept that the uncouth peasant has a great deal of common sense and a capacity to learn, frequently even more than is displayed by his social superiors. This view is particularly evident half a century later in Antonio de Guevara's *Villano del Danubio,* and later in the nineteenth-century Romantic idea of the inherent nobility of the savage who remains unspoiled by civilization. The shepherds are a composite of Salamancan and biblical shepherds. In this way Lucas Fernández helped to consolidate the secular drama with that which had relied on religious inspiration. He and the other so-called "primitive" Spanish playwrights produced a fusion of the profane and the religious elements of drama. The anachronistic interplay of the biblical and the coetaneous shepherds is increased by the mention of other postbiblical Christian elements as the clergy (*Farsas*, p. 143, v. 154) and the canonized saints, Paul and Ana (p. 147, vv. 294, 299).

In this play as in the later *Auto pastoril castellano* by Gil Vicente, the shepherd who speaks of the birth of Christ and the prophecies made of it is used also for purposes of contrast with his other rustic companions. Although he is of low origin like his less learned friends, it is nonetheless he, as one of them, who elaborates on the meaning of the holy event. It is as if, in a sense, he had been suddenly touched by divine inspiration or illumined by the Holy Ghost. In Juan's case, as opposed to the case of the learned Macario in the preceding play, it is not a question of learning or of a higher social status so much as of a personal temperament and disposition of the individual that justifies his uncommon knowledge.

The picaresque element in the play is negligible, but the development of the comic personage as a type is seen to be well under way, since Lloreynte has several traits that are characteristic of the *gracioso* who is later to become a stylized comic character: Lloreynte is lazy and displays the gluttony for which the *gracioso* is famous. Lloreynte overeats and when he is asked to start the concluding song of the play, he excuses himself: "I, by my faith, will not sing/ for I'm so overstuffed with garlic,/ that I'm choking with saliva,/ and I won't be able to talk!" (pp. 152–53, vv. 532–35). Moreover, inasmuch as Lloreynte is incapable of singing because he is so stuffed with food, he must "locate a replacement, since four shepherds are needed to sing the *villancico*." [9] Charlotte Stern has pointed out that this incident involving the concordant arrangement for a singing performance, "calls attention to the polyphony practiced by the Renaissance shepherds." [10] She further reasons at this that the truly popular tradition of the *villancico* was monodic, consequently the musical compositions of Fernández in polyphonic arrangements show "the influence of the Renaissance on the poets and musicians of the Spanish Court who cultivated the literary Christmas play." [11]

In addition to the polyphonic song near the end, we also have another instance of Fernández' innovating useful stage directions that announce a dance which is to accompany the singing: "A *villancico* for a singing and dancing exit" (p. 154, v. 585). The play ends in a clamor as the entire meadow lights up to music and song: "Let's enjoy a thousand joys,/ make a thousand dance steps,/ sing a thousand songs/ and a thousand joyful sounds" (p. 154, vv. 572–75).

For dating this play, we can make use only of the following data: In 1502 Gil Vicente follows the same pattern of revelation by a shepherd in his *Auto pastoril castellano* as we see in this play by Lucas Fernández. Assuming precedence for Lucas' play, the year for its composition would come before 1502, but probably no earlier than 1500. We surmise the latter date by interpreting the line, *También pudo parir Juana* ("Joan also was able to give birth"), (p. 147, v. 300), as a likely reference to the second daughter of the Catholic Kings, *Juana la Loca* (Joan the Mad), 1497–1555, who gave birth to the future Charles I of Spain in February of 1500 in Ghent, Belgium.

CHAPTER 10

Sources and Influences

A S happens in so many works of literature, many paths, sources, and influences crisscross, intermingle, and fuse in the works of Lucas Fernández as well. Classical, Medieval, Renaissance, religious, and profane influences come together in the work of Lucas Fernández and each leaves its indelible mark. Yet the most prevalent and most direct influence is that which is the result of Lucas' close professional relationship with Juan del Encina, whose poetic and dramatic theories he followed rigorously. Encina, despite the personal defects that he may have had, was a highly creative poet who boasted of learned and influential friends, and who was a man of uncommon learning and talent. He was a friend of Antonio de Nebrija, as the latter himself writes,[1] and a great admirer of Juan de Mena, the most esteemed Spanish poet of the fifteenth century, indeed more esteemed by other contemporary poets than was the Marqués de Santillana or Jorge Manrique.

Juan del Encina seemed to have been thoroughly conscious of the need to create diversionary events for the general public. Now that the Spanish wars of reconquest had ended, *ya no nos falta de buscar sino escoger en qué gastemos el tiempo pues lo tenemos cual lo deseamos* ("we no longer need to seek, but to choose in what to spend our time, since we have as much of it as we want").[2] He, for one, felt that he could answer the call from his countrymen in providing them with entertainment. Lucas Fernández, on his part, seems to have held a similar belief.

It cannot be denied that Lucas Fernández owes a debt of literary influence to the restless Encina. There is no doubt that both of these talented writers collaborated quite closely on some of their plays, particularly those of Encina which were presented in the ducal court of Alba. Their dramas may also have been presented in some royal palace of Salamanca, where from time to time the ruling family would make its appearance in the university city. It is very possible, too, that Lucas, initially as an understudy of Encina, acted in some of the latter's plays. This apprenticeship served him in good stead. As an actor, after having memorized many of the lines of the plays, and therefore having become thoroughly familiar with their plot and technique, it was no great feat for Lucas to combine his acquired knowledge with his natural talent and thus use it in composing his own plays. In this manner he became a full-fledged competitor to Encina, rather than merely continuing as his modest understudy. As a matter of fact, as we have seen, he was able to improve upon his mentor in several instances.

To be more specific, to what extent was Lucas Fernández a disciple and imitator of Juan del Encina, and how was this imitation manifested in his works? Thematic indebtedness is surely the most easily detectable of all, but this does not mean that the imitation was slavish. The prevalent themes of pastoral love as a parody of courtly love and the celebrated Nativity theme were already traditional ones. Rather limited in scope, they were treated much in the same way by virtually all the Spanish Renaissance dramatists, starting as early as the fifteenth century with Gómez Manrique and continuing to the period of Lope de Rueda (1505?–1565), who began to embark on somewhat radical tangents from the age-old and much used thematic material. In Lucas' day the learned, active dramatists concentrated on the subjects of the Nativity, the commemorative events of the Holy Week, and upon pastoral or rustic scenes which were often done in contrast to the life in the city.

Some critics have belittled the western dialectal usage in Fernández' works, maintaining that he literally borrowed it from Encina. But the tradition of the dialect had been used successfully since the days of Juan Ruiz and his *Libro de buen amor*, in which we find the Archpriest's venturesome, but fictional, encounters with the aggressively crude highland girls. Using rustic language for comic relief in the early plays was a widespread tactic which Lucas intensified by basing the literary dialect on actual speech.

Encina's shadow casts its nebulous form in diverse configurations on Fernández' work. We have seen some of Encina's techniques used by Fernández in Chapter 5. There is a similarity between the two playwrights in their use of exclamatory words, as is borne out by Encina's *villancico* of the second eclogue and Fernández' first comedy. Encina writes: *¡Nunca tal cosa se vio!/ ¡Huy ho!/ ¡Ni jamás fue ni será!/ ¡Huy ha!* ("Never was such a thing seen!/ Huy ho!/ Neither was nor will be!/ Huy ha!"), (*Églogas,*[3] p. 40). In Fernández, the exclamations appear as: *Ñunca tal fue, ñunca, ño./ ¡Huy ha! ¡Huy ho! ¡He, huy ha!* ("Never was there such a thing, no./ . . . ."), (*Farsas*, p. 74, vv. 622–23). The subject matter of the two songs, however, is different. In one case it applies to the birth of Christ, and in the other to a marriage celebration, but the form of the exclamatory interjections is so close that one cannot help recalling Encina's version upon reading the one by Lucas. There is in each case likewise an undercurrent of bubbling joy expressed by both songs.

We have already observed that Lucas was intimately familiar with the technique of plot and that he sustained a thorough knowledge of characters from Encina's plays. This is made evident by his own citation of Encina's works in his *Farce of Prabos and the Soldier,* which we discussed in Chapter 6.

But it was not only Encina's drama that offered a source for Lucas while he was forming the ideas and techniques for his own subsequent works; he utilized other art forms as well. The songs and poems of Encina that appeared in his *Cancionero* of 1496 were an easily accessible and rich fountain of ideas. The enumerations of the wedding presents which appear in their rudimentary form in the *serranillas* of Juan Ruiz, and are later developed by Lucas Fernández, also appear in a 180-line poem by Encina entitled "Almoneda" ("Auction"). This poem contains a lengthy list of varied things being sold by a would-be student, hopeful of getting into the University of Bologna. Similar lists were later used in equally limitless recitations of the dowries in the marriage plays by the early Spanish dramatists. Encina's humorous cataloguing of the student's personal effects (*Cancionero,* fol. lvi. v°) finds another parallel in the personal and household items with specific application to the dowry which is listed in a dialogued *villancico* also by Encina (*Cancionero,* fol. c r°). In this song Mingo, the groom, is questioned by his master, who will be the sponsor of the wedding, about Mingo's marriage to a *serrana,* and about the dowry which she brings with her to him and the gifts that he gives to her. The extensive list is found in the song entitled *Ya soy desposado/ nuestramo,/ ya soy desposado* ("I'm already married,/ my lord, I'm already married"). Its 304 lines obviously portend the later narrations of dowries and gifts that the rustics enumerate before their wedding celebrations in the marriage plays of the century. Some lines of this dialogued song will give a sampling of the list: *¿No te dan con esso/ otra res alguna?/ —Vn burro bien gruesso/ y una res porcuna;/ y aun otra ovejuna . . . / . . . / —Y darte han almario,/ arca y espetera/ y aun de buen donario/ y trulla y caldera:/ olla y cobertera* ("Don't they give you with that/ some other stock?/ —A nice and fat donkey/ and a swine/ and even a sheep/ . . . / . . . / —And they ought to give you a cabinet, chest and a rack/ and even of good giving/ and a trowel and cauldron/ kettle and potlid") (*Cancionero*, fols. c r°, ci r°).

And a *villancico* that deals with disenchanted love serves congruently with plays on the same subject as an evident thematic inspiration for Lucas Fernández. His profane plays and his *Dialogue for Singing* hinge on this very subject. The *villancico* by Encina is entitled *Dime, Juan, por tu salud/ pues te picas de amorío si es mal de amor el mío* ("Tell me, Juan, by your health/ since you boast of love/ whether my illness is lovesickness"), (*Cancionero*, fol. cii r°). One of the strophes reads as follows: *Percançó me esta passión/ el día de la velada/ oteando a mi adamada/ aquella del Torrejón:/ do sentí tal turbación/ que de mí ya desconfío/ si es mal de amor el mío* ("This passion caught me/ the day of the wake/ looking at my beloved/ the one from Torrejón/ where I felt such confusion/ that I have no hope for me/ whether my illness is lovesickness"), (*Ibid.*).

Finally, the dramatic formula used by Fernández in his *farsas* was closely analogous to the one used by Encina in his *églogas*. Encina in turn had picked it up from his other colleagues and forerunners in the theater. Some of this theatrical influence came from abroad, perhaps from Italy, as had also the Spanish poetic foundation. The theater in Italy, after all, was further along in its development in the vernacular (e.g., that of Machiavelli) than it was in Spain, where the Spanish authors were awakening to its vast possibilities and to their own potential in it.

Fernández, of course, made his own important contributions to the theater. The items discussed above are developed by him in certain ways beyond their form or content as found in Encina's *Cancionero*. For example, the *villancico* in Encina which is actually a dialogue-song, but with no clear-cut indications of speakers, becomes a song-drama in Fernández' hands with precise assignation of the speeches to different singer-actors. The love theme which is not entirely developed by Encina is elaborated and expanded by Fernández into a well-balanced dramatic piece. In his role as understudy and collaborator with Encina, Fernández was afforded a tremendous opportunity by which to profit. Fortunately for the Spanish stage, he took full advantage of it.

All in all, as is to be expected, there are similarities and differences between the two poets. Lucas is more theologically minded than Encina, while the latter is more materialistic, and both of them shared the same inclination in many respects toward didacticism. Encina's materialistic philosophy can best be summarized in one of his most famous of the lasting refrains: *que todos hoy nos hartemos/ que mañana ayunaremos* ("let us all stuff ourselves today,/ for tomorrow we will go hungry"), (*Eglogas,* p. 90).

Lucas was a keen observer of man and an experienced manipulator of artistic conventions. He succeeded in expressing the essence of love without romantic excesses, just as he could express the pathos of the suffering Christ in his *Passion Play* without resorting to extravagant exaggerations. With good reason Cañete considered him the Calderón of early Spanish dramatic literature (Cañete, p. lxx), while Valbuena Prat sees in Fernández' composition the same plastic technique used by Van der Weyden in his characteristic expressions of the true essence of events and actions.[4]

The tendency to name characters according to their personal physical or circumstantial characteristics is something that appears with some consistency in Lucas Fernández and Juan del Encina. We find names like Miguel Turra (*turrón,* "sinecure," or *turrión,* "twist"), Juan Benito ("blessed" because things turn out well for him), Bonifacio ("good doer"), Macario ("happy"), a bona fide name but applicable to the same state of mind, and in Encina this type of naming appears as in Fileno ("delicate, loving") and develops into a true comic device with Piernicurto ("short legged").

I *Other Influences on Fernández*

Naturally, there were other influences that affected Lucas Fernández besides the ones noted from Encina. We have had occasion earlier to refer to his mention of the bawd, Celestina. Yet the occasional similarities found every now and then between the great literary masterpiece of Fernando de Rojas and the dramas of our author are not necessarily direct. In many instances the similarities are simply due to the general thought processes of the day. In the *Celestina* (ed., Cejador y Frauca, II, 34–35), for example, we have the democratic viewpoint brought forth concerning the idea that all humans are children of Adam and Eve. In Lucas Fernández the shepherds insist that *Todos somos de un terruño* ("We are all of the same clay"), (*Farsas,* p. 126, v. 212).

Another favorite device which can be traced to traditional influences is the poetic pitting of opposites against each other, that is, the idea that opposites balance, nullify, and therefore "cure" each other: cold overcomes heat and vice versa, love cures hate and vice versa. This idea is exploited repeatedly in the plays of Lucas. The juxtaposition of unexpected words recalls the very same devices proposed by Petrarch. But naturally, although these literary tricks seem to be noticed first in Petrarch among the writers of the Romance languages, their existence is, as in most such literary instances, an ancient one and can be traced to the writings on practical philosophy to Aristotle's pursuit of truth in his *Rhetoric.* The use of opposites was extensively known in the Renaissance period, and even prior to that, as a reading of the Archpriest of Talavera's (Alfonso Martínez de Toledo's) *Corbacho* shows, when he mentions Aristotle precisely in conjunction with the use of opposites (Chapter XVI). Martínez designates Aristotle as the originator of the idea of opposites, at least for existing Western literature.

The *Dialogue for Singing* has as its central motive the exposure of the ills of love. It shows that the author understood them so well that he may have experienced them himself. No doubt he also could hear, read, or see the effects of love all around him. His sensitive definitions of love show that he knew it well. Definitions of love as that expressed by Lucas were made in a popular traditional vein and are traceable to the *Libro de buen amor* for

Spanish literature. The definition of love and the tirades against
it, which were a standard medieval practice in Spain, quite certainly had at least part of their origin in Ovid's own tirade against
love in his *Remedia amoris (Remedies of Love)* which was appended to his *Ars amatoria (Art of Love)*. The subject matter of
love continued to be nourished on Spanish soil and emerges in
a prose work dating from about 1513, *Questión de amor (Question of Love)*.[5] It is treated in very much the same lyrical vein
in which it persists in our dramatist.

The oxymoronic effect, which we find used very effectively in
the *Passion Play* as in the phrase *dulce lamentar* (sweet lamenting) was another standard device in the Medieval Ages. In the
Celestina we find this practice with a parallel reference to love:
*vna agradable llaga, vn sabroso veneno, vna dulce amargura, vna
delectable dolencia, vn alegre tormento, vna dulce e fiera herida,
vna blanda muerte* ("an agreeable wound, a tasty venom, a
sweet bitterness, a delectable pain, a happy torment, a sweet and
fierce wound, a soft death").[6] The same contradictory usage of
terms provides a similar effect in Juan Ruiz' poem *De la Pasión de
Nuestro Señor Jesuxristo* in which he speaks of *Las llagas . . .
[que] son más dulces* ("The wounds [that] are sweeter").[7] We
have noticed a number of times that there are inescapable reminiscences of lines showing Lucas' indebtedness to the *Libro de
buen amor*. This is especially true for the opening monologue
which sets the scene of a cold day (*Farsas*, p. 140); it is much
the same type of setting as Juan Ruiz' protagonist encountered
while traveling in the wintry hills of the Guadarrama range.

Although Fernández only occasionally surpassed the poetic
heights of Encina, as in the *Passion Play* or the *Farce of Prabos*,
he was considerably more original in the use of natural dialogue
and local dialect for the purpose of characterization. From the
point of view of dramatic content and expression, particularly
in the aforementioned *Passion Play*, Lucas also is unexcelled. It
was he who served as a link between Encina and the later playwrights, Torres Naharro and Gil Vicente. There are several scenes
in all these dramatists' works which bear tantalizing resemblances.
Vicente was incontrovertibly directly indebted to Fernández for
his second dramatic effort and first bona fide play, *Auto pastoril
castellano* (1502). Indeed, the tradition of the rustic dialect used

for comic effect in the Golden Age Spanish drama itself received
its greatest impetus from Lucas Fernández.

II   *The Influence of Lucas Fernández on Others*

Although an earlier chapter presented some of the influences
that Lucas had upon Gil Vicente, herewith a more intensive
treatment of these will be given. The second dramatic effort by
Vicente shows unmistakable borrowings from the first comedy
written by Lucas in 1496. There is perhaps a vague influence
of Encina in Vicente's play, but that which derives from Fernández is very specific. It is clearly brought out by the genealogical
recitations of the shepherds in the related plays of Fernández and
Vicente. In his *Comedy,* Fernández has Bras Gil defend his right
to marry his beloved when he is confronted by her grandfather's
objections which insinuate that Bras Gil comes of inferior family
stock. In his contention that he descends from good ancestral
lineage, Bras Gil names *Papiharto* as a cousin, and lists *Juan de
los Bodonales* among his kinfolk, then adds *Espulgazorras* among
several others (*Farsas,* p. 70). Gil Vicente incorporates some of
the ideas of the passage which contains these names into a similar
but enlarged piece in his own play in which Gil, an alter ego of
Vicente, recites the family background of his friend's wife. The
words *Papiharto, Bodonales* and *Espulgazorras* stand out prominently to mark their source.[8] In the corresponding passages there
are other phrases which suggest Fernández as a source for Vicente's play: *son mis primos caronales* ("they are my blood
cousins") in Fernández, becomes *son sus primos caronales* ("they
are her blood cousins") in Vicente; and elsewhere in the drama
we read, *el crego de Vico-Nuño,/ que es vn hombre bien sesudo*
("the priest from Vico- Nuño/ who is quite a wise man"), (*Farsas,* p. 70, vv. 447–48) from Fernández, leaves this impression on
Vicente: *El crego de Bico-Nuño/ te enseñó esso al domingo*
("the priest from Vico-Nuño taught you that on Sunday"),
(*Vicente,* p. 10). In another case of the *Auto pastoril castellano,*
where Vicente requires several pastoral names, Fernández' line
sobrino de Juan Jarrete ("nephew of Juan Jarrete"), (*Farsas,*
p. 70, v. 439), serves Vicente as *¡Ah, Jarrete! ¡Ah, Bras Juan!*
("Hey, Jarrete! Hey, Bras Juan!"), (*Vicente,* p. 12). No other
one of the early dramatists makes use of the particular names

cited here, nor are they common elsewhere; the noted relationship here between the two works is thus justified.

The rustic dowry which the grandfather of Beringuella offers with her in marriage (*Farsas*, p. 71) contains the usual accouterments for the kitchen, as *vasar* (shelving), *espetera* (rack), and the indispensable *cama* (bed), and the livestock as *burro* (donkey), *res porcuna* (pig), and *vaca* (cow), etc., are clearly recalled in the passage by Vicente (*Vicente*, p. 15) in which Silvestre, the newly married shepherd, tells of the dowry his bride brings to him. Besides Vicente, Torres Naharro also made use of this type of material in the *introito* to the *Diálogo del nascimiento* where the shepherd speaks of the property he will receive with the bride. There, the common words that appear in Fernández' play (*Farsas*, pp. 71–72) and that are shared by Torres Naharro include *almadraque* (mattress), *cencerro* (cowbell), *perro* (dog), (*Propalladia*, I, 263). These dowry recitations appeared earlier relegated only to poems as found in Juan Ruiz and Juan del Encina, but they were introduced into the Spanish vernacular drama judging by the evidence at hand, first by Fernández; after him, the dowry recitations soon became a convention of the early Spanish theater.

Textual and thematic parallelism is also remarkably impressive in Vicente's *Auto da alma* (*ca.* 1517) which reveals telling traces of Fernández' *Passion Play* (*ca.* 1503). The disparity between the dates of these works is overcome by the recollection that in this case Vicente may have used as a model the published form of the play (1514) by Fernández. The reference in his letter to John III of Portugal about his colleague's published works, which he had seen, may in this case be perfectly applicable as an explanation for the apparent parallels.

In addition to the *Comedy*, still another play, the *Play of the Nativity* (1500–1502) by Fernández may have had some connection, though less clearcut, with Vicente's *Auto pastoril castellano*. In both Nativity plays the authors cite the biblical figure, Malachi, who makes the prophecy on the birth of Christ and on the devastation that will befall Jerusalem. This is not used by other early Spanish dramatists and hence claim of some relationship by the two is probable.

As we saw in an earlier chapter, the personal elements disclosed in the *Auto pastoril castellano* by Vicente would indicate that Lucas Fernández took an active part in the production of Vicente's second stage effort and that the two dramatists were close collaborators in the early days of the Iberian theater.[9]

Though mutual influence among the foregoing dramatists on various topics is clear and unmistakable, there is no evidence of identical passages that would argue for outright plagiarism in any one author. This demonstrates that they were sufficiently familiar with each other's works to be able to quote an occasional line and to remember the general structure of a play without the necessity of actually consulting a manuscript or a printed text of it.

III *The Innovations*

When Lucas Fernández entered the ranks of the Spanish dramatists, Juan del Encina had already published his *Cancionero*. Lucas, as we have seen, learned much from his tutor regarding the technique of the then nascent Spanish vernacular theater, and subsequently he was able to make his own contributions in the development of this genre. For example, although the use of rustic dialects had been appearing in Castilian literature as a humorous device since the days of the *Libro de buen amor,* the dialects had little basis in actual local speech. As we saw in Chapter 5, Lucas profoundly altered the course of the rustic dialects by taking the local Salamancan speech (properly called *charro,* but nowadays known by the misnomer of *sayagués*), and by placing its characteristics in a definitely important position in his plays. Thus he injected an earthy, racy humor into them. In establishing a firm foundation for this type of humor, he was following a technique already generally known and accepted and expressed earlier by Fray Iñigo de Mendoza, who used dialectal humor in his plays, in order to keep interest alive in the audience and in the reader.[10]

Shergold has pointed out that Lucas was conscious of the new Italian drama and attempted to associate some of his plays with it by giving them the name *farsa o cuasi comedia;* [11] yet in spite of this awareness of the variegated offering of the flourishing Italian theater, his own remained focused on the pastoral tradition as did that of Encina. Although Encina's *Égloga XIV* of Plácida and Vitoriano is termed a *commedia* in a contemporary report of its performance in Rome (1513), it is, like Lucas' plays, also in a pastoral tradition. It seems, therefore, that Fernández and Encina preferred this tradition and yet had some indebtedness to the Italian comedy. It was Lucas who was the innovator in being the first of the early Spanish playwrights to appropriate the Italian designation for plays and so to refer to his own plays as *comedias*. This classifying term was subsequently popularized in the Golden Age theater, even in the face of the fact that other terms like *auto* had previously been used as early as the *Auto de los Reyes Magos* (twelfth century); Encina, as has been stated, used *égloga* or *representación*, and while Fernando de Rojas utilized *tragicomedia*, Bartolomé de Torres Naharro accepted *comedia*. It should also be noted that while Lucas was groping for direction, he likewise used such composite phrases as *auto o farsa* or *égloga o farsa* and finally *farsa o comedia*, besides the simple terms of *auto* and *comedia*, which he used independently of others. The concurrent vacillation in terminology for the dramatized pieces is symptomatic of the uncertainty felt about aspects of the nascent literary genre in the Spanish vernacular. Ultimately, the term which became crystallized in the popular mind was *comedia*, which came to encompass all productions, whether they were of a tragic or comic nature.

The evolving vernacular theater received yet another momentous boost from Lucas in the form of the opening speeches made in each of his plays. Although the fourth play, the *Play of the Nativity*, has been generally singled out by critics as the first one to use the introductory *introito* practiced later by Torres Naharro, the introductory lines at the rising of the curtain are a normal procedure in Lucas Fernández' works and are present in each of his plays except the *Maiden's Farce*. The character of the initial scenes of the plays merely gives the background and setting of the action but provides no indication of the plot which is to follow. After his exposition, he remains on stage to join forces in the action with the other characters. Torres Naharro picked up where Lucas left off and deliberately separated the *introito* from the rest of the play and made it into a preface. The rustic who recited the *introito* of Torres Naharro's dramas had a function somewhat like that of a master of ceremonies and did not necessarily enter into the performance that followed, although at times he did.

Torres Naharro used Lucas Fernández as a source for other

ideas. In the *Diálogo del nascimiento*, Patrispano is modeled on Lucas' Macario.[12] In fact, the entire *Diálogo del nascimiento* is patterned on Lucas' *Play of the Nativity*. Professor Gillet dates the play by Torres Naharro as early as 1504. The *Play of the Nativity* by Lucas is from about 1500. Both the plays are largely theological and discursive in content, and both are full of a coarse humor conveyed largely in rustic dialect.

Laurence Keates, as others, has discussed the transference of ideas among the various early dramatists. He indicates that: "From Lucas Fernández [*The Maiden's Farce*], rather than from Encina, it is probably that Vicente took the idea that love is a great leveller, and that a nobleman may well love a maid of low birth. This is the theme of *Comedia do Viuvo;* it figures also in the *Rubena*, and there are echoes in *D. Duardos*." [13]

Keates maintains moreover that "Fernández also preceded Vicente, in the *Farsa del Nascimiento de Nuestro Señor Jesucristo* [which we call the *Play of the Nativity*] in a realization of the rigours of the weather, especially in winter, as shown in Pascual's semi-blasphemous plaints." [14] It was only later in his life that Vicente definitely forsook the idyllic pastoral denouement for the realistic one.

Lucas Fernández with his innovations thus helped to enrich both the Spanish and Portuguese dramatic offerings. Still another tangible influence was wrought by Fernández on Fray Antonio de Guevara (1480–1545), who was six years younger than Lucas and appears to have been a staunch companion to Prince Juan in the court of the Catholic Kings. Guevara's distinct indebtedness to the Salamancan author is perceptible most notably in the essay called *Monte Calvario*, very similar in its rending, emotional tones to Lucas' *Passion Play*. The resemblance is heightened by the fact that Guevara's piece is also written in verse. It is intensely dramatic in spite of the lack of action. The drama is created here, as in Fernández' piece, through skillful narration. The key words in both works are *lágrimas* (tears) and *sangre* (blood), and both are in a way somewhat related even to the current of strong emotion that runs through the sentimental novels. The style of this work by Antonio de Guevara is such that it appears to be directly inspired by Lucas' play, yet how can such parallelism be rationalized? Perhaps by noting that it stems from Guevara's relationship with Prince Juan. As a companion to the Prince, Antonio de Guevara would have had as much access to the plays performed by Lucas Fernández (and by others) as had the Prince himself. The influence from Fernández which we observe in Guevara's work is therefore altogether probable.

Noted earlier was the Romantic idea of the noble savage rooted in early religions and found in Lucas Fernández in its earliest Spanish form. Here the nobility of the humble shepherd is celebrated alongside that of the courtier. This finds broader elaboration in Guevara, and later on the thought was embellished considerably in the *Fables* of the Frenchman, La Fontaine (1621–1695): *Fable XI*, 7: *Le Paysan du Danube*. Hence, to repeat, some of the notable currents manifest in Lucas Fernández were revived by Fray Antonio de Guevara. Inasmuch as the latter holds a place of importance in universal literary circles through his widely known *Reloj de príncipes* and the fantastically popular *Epístolas familiares*, the importance of Lucas Fernández acquires new dimensions, since the works by Guevara served as thematic and stylistic inspiration in much of Western literature.

IV *The Shepherd as Forerunner of the* Gracioso

Another important aspect of the early theater remains to be mentioned: the shepherd as a forerunner of the comic characters, the *bobo* and the *gracioso:* the latter by the time of Lope de Vega had become the stock comic type of the Golden Age drama. The shepherd's mischievous wit and ironic humor bear a striking resemblance particularly to this comic type. The characteristics of the comic shepherd of the sixteenth century include cowardice, sluggishness, gluttony, boastfulness at his expertness in various rustic tasks, together with such worthy accomplishments as the ability to play the flute, to dance, to jump, and even to wrestle. The latter series of attributes, however, is seldom seen in the *gracioso*.

These conditions of temperament appear very early in the Spanish vernacular drama, and most can be traced to the episode of the traveler in Juan Ruiz' *Libro de buen amor*, which describes his encounter with the mountain girl who believed him to be a shepherd (strophes 993 to 1042). It can be seen, then, that the comic rustic type has a long history and issues from a rich liturgical and literary tradition. The theater, after all, always has had some sort of comic personage to delight the audiences. The medieval plays often had the devil as a comic figure, while the *Auto de los Reyes Magos* has a comic, blustering character in Herod. By the middle of the fifteenth century, it was the stage shepherds who were saying silly and insolent things to make their spectators laugh.

The Golden Age *gracioso*'s inclination to indolence and sleep is a trait also well brought out in Gil's personality of the *Play of the Nativity*. When Gil abruptly cuts Bonifacio short in the recitation of his ancestors, *¡A ruyn seas tú y tus parientes!* ("The devil with you and your relatives!"), Bonifacio counters, *¿Tienes tú otros mijores?* ("Do you have better ones?"). But this, instead of stirring up a long harangue from Gil, only evokes a philosophical thought, and a short one, because he claims to be too sleepy to make it long. He withdraws by saying, *quédate a Dios, que vn sueño/ vo a dormir tras vn carrasco* ("good bye, for I'm going/ to take forty winks behind an oak"), (*Farsas*, p. 126).

The *gracioso*'s typical cowardice had its forerunner in the shepherd of the *Maiden's Farce:* while maintaining his right to love a damsel, he argues with the cavalier, whereupon the latter threatens him with his sword, and then the terror-stricken shepherd pleads, *Dexá, dexá la joyosa/ la grimosa/ no la saquéys* ("Leave, leave the sword/ the sad one/ don't draw it"), (p. 91, vv. 430–32).

The same rustic's tenacious but fruitless courtship of a damsel, meant by the author as a mockery of courtly love, is a model for the later *gracioso*'s often awkward but sensuous lovemaking which symmetrically balances the loftier amorous affairs of his master in the drama of the seventeenth century. Along the same lines, in the *Farce of Prabos* Pascual audaciously denounces the soldiery for their overwhelming self-righteousness; brought up short by the soldier's quick anger at his insults, he falls back to timidity and meekness when the opportunity to retreat affords itself. He assures the soldier that what he has said, *por prazer lo hazía* ("I was just kidding"), (p. 111, v. 573).

Pascual of the *Play of the Nativity* is likewise seen as a budding *gracioso* as he proclaims his sluggishness and thoughts about food: *Quiérome aquí rellanar,/ con gozo prazentero/ como zagal costumero* ("I want to lie here,/ with pleasing joy/ as a sluggish lad"), (p. 319, vv. 16–18), and *Digo que de aquí adelante/*

quiero andar más perpujante;/ comer, beber de contino,/ tassajo, soma y buen vino ("I say that from now on/ I want to be more stout,/ eat, drink constantly/ beef, bread and good wine"), (p. 140, vv. 24–27). In the same play, Lloreynte is depicted as a composite of the comic character's stereotyped individuality. He is gluttonous, sleepy, ingenuous, and yet filled with common sense.

The shepherds of the semireligious *Play of the Nativity* are less sensuous than they are in the strictly secular plays of Fernández, or in those by Encina; and they are not quite as scatologically inclined as those of Bartolomé de Torres Naharro. Generally speaking, Fernández' shepherds bear a greater similarity in their nature and comic temperament to those of Gil Vicente than they do to the shepherds of the other playwrights, though they are not quite as jocose as are those of the Portuguese dramatist. The latter's rustics perhaps remain the most adroitly handled from a comic point of view; their original inspiration evidently stems from the shepherds of Fernández.

The mixture of the serious and the burlesque is a timeworn convention in the theater. The humorous scenes in Lucas Fernández' plays, therefore, are usually an integral and inseparable portion of the works in which they appear, whether they be injected as complete units in themselves or interspersed as scattered questions and answers among the interlocutors. Such an alternation of the sublime and the ridiculous is a psychological necessity contrived by the dramatist in order to release the tensions and emotions he creates in his audience through the action on stage.

CHAPTER 11

Summation

IN the preceding chapters we noticed both the several influences that acted upon Lucas Fernández' literary production
and the artistic contributions that he himself made to the Spanish
vernacular theater. The rise of drama as a literary genre in the
Spanish tongue was a very complicated phenomenon. Its origin
cannot be sought in a unique point of genesis. It was rather the
result of polygenesis, of complex interrelationships among several
types of public entertainment which were then being staged—
among them Classical and medieval Latin drama, comic skits
and sung playlets, both in Latin and the vernacular. The medieval
actors and entertainers, commonly known as minstrels, were
responsible in large measure for the preservation of the musical
and histrionic art as well as for its adaptation to the exigencies
of the audiences of the day. Thus the vernacular requirements
molded and adjusted the existing public diversions to produce
the Renaissance Spanish drama that in the following centuries
blossomed into the national theater known as Golden Age Drama.

Lucas Fernández' contributions to the vernacular theater were
made at a time when printing by movable type had already been
introduced to Spain. He came at a point of history when the
Church was openly interested in encouraging performances of
many types of plays. Its attitude of condemnation of such public
entertainment had changed. The Church throughout its history
had alternately both condemned and condoned the theater. At
the end of the fifteenth and the beginning of the sixteenth centuries the Church, in giving its blessing, fostered the dramatic talents
of its many adherents. With a favorable atmosphere, coupled
with technical advantages working in their favor, some of the
Spanish dramatists, such as Iñigo de Mendoza and Juan del Encina, had already made successful efforts to have their works
published. Mendoza's *Vita Christi* was in fact among the first

works thus honored in Spanish by the Catholic Kings, who supported its publication. These authors, Mendoza and Encina, were among the first to have their Spanish plays printed in numerous copies which permitted the survival of isolated texts. Earlier attempts at popular theater without the preservative help of the printing press and a benevolent Church have in most instances vanished with the ages. Fernández followed the example of Encina and Mendoza, and compiled some of his own plays which he published in his hometown of Salamanca in the year 1514. He was perhaps then at the most vigorous period of his life, planning entertainments for Spanish royalty, serving as organist in the chapel of Queen María of Portugal, managing real estate as a businessman, and tending to the spiritual needs of his flock as a priest in Salamanca and in the neighboring localities. The multiplicity of his interests took him on trips outside of Spain to Portugal before he finally settled down for the remainder of his life to the duties of a professor of music at the University of Salamanca.

Of the several playwrights who survive in print from the early Peninsular theater in the vernacular language, Lucas Fernández remained a major link that had been for some time left unexplored. Nonetheless, his name figures repeatedly in histories dealing with Spanish drama and literature. Various editions have been made of some of his plays, or portions of them, over the centuries, while two editions of his complete plays have appeared after the princeps edition of 1514. Recent studies on the playwrights of the sixteenth century have helped to set into place the pieces of the puzzle on the early Spanish dramatic literature. The studies reveal that the early playwrights had a considerable amount of knowledge of each other's works, and that they were well aware of the tendencies going on in their day in this ever-popular field of public entertainment. Their awareness of each other's activities appears to have extended on occasion to seeing each other's plays and even participating in them.

Just as the nobility, the businessmen, the clerics, and the academes kept up with events in their particular lines of endeavor, thus the early Peninsular playwrights stayed abreast of the advances in their own field and managed to exchange information concerning the techniques and devices of the theater. As early as the last decade of the fifteenth century, there were groups of entertainers in Spain who performed together so often, on so many different occasions and in so many different places, that they could pass for professionals in every respect, even though perhaps they were not then labeled as such. These groups of players, perhaps to be termed semiprofessionals for the lack of a more precise term, would be engaged by individuals of the nobility, by church chapters, or by government officials for performances in palaces, in courtyards, church cloisters, and public squares. Lucas Fernández apparently participated in and played with just such a histrionic group. He was probably a budding actor even while he attended the University of Salamanca as a student. Later he not only acted in the plays of other writers, but also wrote them on his own under the auspices of the Duke of Alba, the Church, the Royal Spanish household, and the city and university community. He followed the Spanish royalty to Portugal when the ruling families of the two countries were joined through marriage. He had ample opportunities to present his plays in the bilingual Portuguese court. Whereas in Salamanca and Alba de Tormes he collaborated with Juan del Encina, in Portugal he became closely associated with Gil Vicente.

His plays are known as farces and eclogues, but he also designated them in some cases as acts and comedies. His six extant plays were written between the years 1496 and 1503. Three of the plays are secular, and are considered to be wedding plays, because they were probably presented at wedding celebrations, while the two semireligious dramas were written to commemorate the birth of Christ, and one final play is entirely religious, being devoted to the Crucifixion. They are found in various forms with a preference for the *redondilla*. The plays are characterized primarily by simple, colloquial language. Five of the plays contain linguistic elements with deep-rooted rustic traditions belonging to western Spain, while the sixth is a sacramental play manifesting an elevated, ennobled language and a strongly lyrical style. Here, though the language is refined, it is also clear and simple. An additional seventh play is in reality a musical dialogue presenting a lament of unrequited love. Unfortunately no musical notations have been saved for this Renaissance song-drama which constitutes a forerunner of the contemporary *zarzuela* (musical play). Indeed, it may very well be a continuation from medieval Latin musical plays as *The Play of Daniel*, that was composed in southern France perhaps in the thirteenth century. This type of drama descends linearly to our modern opera.

Fernández' plays are highlighted with songs and dances. These sometimes appear in the midst of the plays and invariably at their conclusions. These musical interludes added an element of variety to the dialogue and action taking place on the stage.

Fernández' productions reveal both a medieval and a Renaissance approach to dramatic trends. His theater already contains the germs of the themes of love, honor, and democratic sentiment, as well as the idea of free will in choosing a marriage partner. The religious theme typical of the liturgical drama of the preceding centuries with its church dogma abounds in the Nativity and the Passion plays. These themes become favorites in the plays of the succeeding centuries. The plots are simple, and the plays' endings culminate either in marriage, if it's a secular play, or in a projected visit to the manger, if the play is on the Nativity, or in the Eucharist for the *Passion Play*. Five of the six plays have moments of comedy provided by the antics of rustic characters. Fernández' humor is achieved through the use of plays on words, coarse language which erupts into an occasional vulgarity, and tendencies toward farce with physical beatings of some unfortunate rustic individual. The slapstick routine is an occasional, but sure device in Fernández' comedies. The serious *Passion Play*, on the other hand, is devoid of any type of humor, as it concentrates on the glorification and the significance of the Passion of Christ.

Fernández tends to observe in his plays the unities of time, place, and action. Although the brevity of his pieces affords little opportunity for developing individual characters, the author is able to show them in several moods and with changes of emotions and attitudes. Thus he avoids presenting mere stony stereotypes. When physical movement of a play's actors is to occur that would require a change of scene and thus a break in the unity of place, at that point usually the play ends with merely a suggestion of the forthcoming action that is to take place elsewhere. In this way the unities are observed and the plots remain rudimentary within the limitations of the single acts. The playwright reveals a sense of scene divisions in the plays by having characters already on stage announce the entrance of others who come to participate in the action. He produces local color by depicting scenes of ordinary life among country folk. He portrays the people at play, at their rustic chores, at their encounters with others who pass their way. In particular, he is especially adept at setting down the peculiar linguistic characteristics of the rustic Salamancan dialect, known properly as *charro*, but which has become engrained in literary criticism with the misnomer of *sayagués.*

Fernández' *Passion Play* is inspired in the biblical recounting of the Crucifixion, and was composed for the purpose of moving its spectators to greater devotion in the Faith and to have them partake of the Eucharist that probably followed the play's performance, in all likelihood, in church. It appears to have been presented as part of the Corpus Christi celebrations during Holy Week. The play is considered to be the poetic culmination of the author's dramatic and lyrical efforts. Its lyricism is achieved through various devices such as anaphora, alliteration, internal rhyme, and predominant use of verbs in the infinitive form. It is one of the plays that has retained its original charm for the Spanish public, as the latter continues to witness its performances even today. Religious plays of this nature came to great prominence with the seventeenth-century Pedro Calderón de la Barca. Fernández' play is of such high caliber that it has earned him the reputation as the "Calderón" of the early Spanish theater.

The position of Lucas Fernández among the early Spanish dramatists is an important one. In the Iberian Peninsula's theatrical development, he trod the same artistic paths as did Encina, Gil Vicente, and Torres Naharro. Lucas Fernández shared in much of the theatrical pioneering. Torres Naharro shows an indebtedness to Fernández in his satire of the soldiers in the *Comedia Soldadesca,* as well as in his technique of introductory monologues, the *introitos,* and in the use of the rustic *sayagués* language. Clear-cut similarities are also evident between the *Comedy* by Fernández and the *Auto pastoril castellano* of Gil Vicente. The crystallization of the comic fool, the *gracioso,* with his characteristic gluttony, sluggishness, dim but practical wit; the development of the love and honor themes; the attention and importance given to stage directions and the new nomenclature of the plays—all these can be traced in large measure to Fernández' ingenuity as a dramatist. We have likewise seen the influence he exercised on a work by Antonio de Guevara, whose translated writings in turn anticipated the development of the baroque in England.[1] Lucas Fernández is seen to have made direct contributions to the dramatic tradition of Spanish literature in particular, and, indirectly through other authors, he left his imprint on the broad expanse of world literature as well.

Notes and References

Chapter One

1. Ricardo Espinosa Maeso, "Ensayo biográfico del Maestro Lucas Fernández," *Boletín de la Real Academia Española*, X (1923), 386–424; "Apéndice de documentos," 567–603. Both hereafter referred to as Espinosa.

2. See p. lxx of Cañete's edition of Lucas Fernández, *"Farsas y églogas"* (Madrid: Imprenta Nacional, 1867). We shall refer to this edition as Cañete.

3. Alonso Cortés, N., "Documentos del Maestro Arias Barbosa," *BRAE*, III (1916), 560–62.

4. Lucas Fernández, *Farsas y églogas*, fascimile edition of the princeps of 1514 prepared by Emilio Cotarelo y Mori (Madrid: Real Academia Española, 1929), frontispiece. This edition is hereafter referred to as *Farsas*, ed. Cotarelo.

5. Espinosa, p. 392.

6. *Ibid.*

7. *Ibid.*, p. 393.

8. This has been communicated to us orally by Dr. Ricardo Espinosa Maeso, who has compiled many pages of unpublished information on Salamancan authors, and particularly on Juan del Encina. Students of the early Spanish drama hope that Dr. Espinosa may find it possible to publish this wealth of information.

9. Cañete, p. 8. Professor Castro presented his thesis in a lecture delivered before the Spanish Comedia group of the Modern Language Association at its annual meeting in Washington, D.C., in 1962.

10. There was indeed a wave of conversions for several generations prior to this period and these were intensified with the policies of the Catholic Kings, the establishment of the Inquisition, and the expulsion of non-Christians from Spain. Therefore, it is not surprising that large numbers of *conversos* will be found in all walks of life, including that of the intelligentsia in Spain during this period. Professor Castro is no doubt right part of the time, simply because the events did call for massive conversions of the people.

LUCAS FERNÁNDEZ

11. Espinosa, p. 392.

12. *Ibid.*, document V, 568.

13. The other two uncles, Martín and Juan, had died in 1479 and 1486 respectively.

14. Luis Ortiz Behety, "El teatro de Lucas Fernández," *Boletín de estudios de teatro,* nos. 24–25 (1949), 37, thinks he was ordained priest in 1495. We believe this date is much too early, for nowhere is Lucas spoken of as a cleric before the year 1506.

15. Espinosa, p. 396.

16. The Duke of Alba, besides maintaining a residence in Salamanca, and elsewhere, possessed the immense palace in Alba de Tormes that stood on top of a hill dominating the green valley below, which was irrigated by the River Tormes. The castle is now in ruins, and only one of its seven towers remains standing. In modern times this tower has been known as the "Tower of the Writers," thus commemorating the residence there of Encina, Lucas Fernández, Lope de Vega, Calderón de la Barca, and others who contributed to the entertainment of the people in the palace. But recently the tower has been reestablished as the "Armor Storage Room." It serves as a tourist attraction with newly painted frescoes depicting events of the Renaissance that involved the third Duke of Alba, son of Don Fadrique. It was the latter who employed both Lucas Fernández and Encina. The tower also contains copies of letters and documents that recall its early days of glory.

17. Espinosa, p. 399.

18. *Ibid.*, p. 401.

19. This information was kindly given us by the Rev. Francisco Rodríguez, the present priest in Alaraz.

20. Espinosa, p. 586, document XX.

21. To support the additional chaplain, the verdict added sixty-four bushels of grain (half wheat and half barley or rye), to the payments of the benefice. These were to be paid right after harvest time to the parish priest (Espinosa, p. 409). Grain harvest in Salamanca comes usually in the month of July.

22. Espinosa, p. 409.

23. *Ibid.*, p. 588.

24. *Ibid.*, p. 603.

25. *Ibid.*, p. 594.

26. *Ibid.*, p. 598.

27. Antonio Caetano de Sousa, *Provas da Historia Genealógica da casa Real portugueza,* II, Provas do Liv. IV, no. 65, "Libro dos moradores da casa da Rainha D. Maria, segunda mulher do Senhor Rey D. Manoel, no tempo em que faleceo" (Lisbon, 1742), p. 374.

Notes and References

Under the heading *Moços da capella*, the third name on the list is: *Lucas Fernandes, Castelhano*.

28. The letter of privileges to Lucas Fernández from King Manuel I reads as follows: *Dom Manoell etc. A vos juizos do couto musteiro do bispado do Cojnbra e a todos outros juizos e justiças oficiaes e pesoas de nosos reynos a que o conhecimento desto pertencia per qualequer guisa que seya e que esta nosa carta de priuilegio desta lajadeiro for mostrada, saude.*

Sabede que querẽdo nos fazer graça e merce a Lucas Fernandez, morador en Regoim, termos do dito couto pora canto ora faz e acresçenta ẽ huas suas casas que hy tem pera serẽ stalajems temos por bem e mandamos que daquy em diante seya priuillegiado e escusado etc. ẽ forma dada ẽ Lixboa a xxbiij [28] dias do mes de majo el Rey ho mandou per dom Pedro bispo de Guarda, etc. e per dom Diogo Piynheiro, bispo do Funchall, etc. Diogo Laso [?] a fez ano de jbᶜxb [1515] anos.

("Don Manuel etc. To you, judges in the ministry of the bishopric of Coimbra and to all the other judges and official justices and persons of our kingdoms to whom knowledge be given of this right by whatever means, and to whom our letter of privileges for hotel-keeper be shown, greetings:

"Know ye that we wishing to do favor and grace to Lucas Fernández, inhabitant of Regoim, within the limits of the said [ministry], that whatever now he may do to and enlarge on some of his homes that he has there in order that they be made into hotels, we deem it proper, and we command that henceforth he be [considered] privileged and excused [from] etc. in the manner granted in Lisbon on the 28th day of the month of May, the King so commanded through don Pedro, bishop of Guarda, etc., and through don Diogo Piynheiro, bishop of Funchall, etc. Diogo Laso [name not clearly legible] wrote it [the letter of privilege] in the year of 1515.") [*Chancelaria*, no. R102, de Manuel I, Liv. 11, fol. 111 vº.]

29. Espinosa, p. 412.

30. *Ibid.*

31. Dr. Ricardo Espinosa Maeso, in one of our conversations, stated his conviction that Lucas did not obtain the degree through a public examination, but rather, as was most common, he merely paid for it. We might add that his competence may have already been proved to such an extent that an examination was not called for and the granting of the degree was a mere formality.

32. Espinosa, p. 415.

33. *Ibid.*, p. 417.

34. *Ibid.*, p. 420.

35. *Ibid.*, p. 423.

Chapter Two

1. It is quite probable that Fernández knew Bartolomé de Torres Naharro (d. 1531?) as well. M. Menéndez y Pelayo, *Estudios de crítica literaria* (Madrid, 1920), in his work on "Bartolomé de Torres Naharro," p. 15, insinuates, though half-heartedly, that Juan del Encina may have been writing of Torres Naharro when he speaks of the shepherd, Bartolo, from Extremadura: *¿Quién te arribó por aquí/ tan lagrimoso y tan solo?/ Yo cuidé qu'eras Bartolo,/ un pastor de Extremadura* . . . ("What brought you here so alone and weeping? I thought you were Bartolo, a shepherd from Extremadura.") Like Fernández and Encina, Torres Naharro probably attended the University of Salamanca, and could have been one of the three youths who shared the post of cantor in Salamanca, as the name Bartolomé suggests in the document pertaining to the division of the position.

2. Ricardo Espinosa Maeso, "Nuevos datos biográficos de Juan del Encina," *Boletín de la Real Academia Española*, VIII (1921), 646.

3. Juan del Encina, *Cancionero*, facsimile edition of the first edition of 1496 prepared by E. Cotarelo y Mori (Madrid: *Revista de Archivos, Bobliotecas y Museos*, 1928), fol. vi, r°.

4. Translated from Juan del Enzina, *Églogas*, ed. H. López Morales (Madrid, 1963), p. 25.

5. *Ibid*, pp. 132–33.

6. Ricardo Espinosa Maeso, "Nuevos datos . . . ," *BRAE*, VIII (1921), 649.

7. *Ibid.*, 651.

8. *Ibid.*

9. *Ibid.*

10. Lucas gained employment in the court chapel of María, the third daughter of the Catholic Sovereigns. ("As a musician Lucas Fernández belonged to the chapel of Queen María, the second wife of D. Manuel. See *Historia Genealógica da Casa Real, Provas*, II, 374, a detail which I have noted elsewhere several times, and yet it has not entered into general knowledge.") Our source is C. Michaëlis de Vasconcellos, *Notas Vicentinas* (Lisbon: Rev. "Ocidente," 1949), p. 472, n. 487.

11. Ricardo Espinosa Maeso, "Nuevos datos . . . ," *BRAE*, VIII (1921), 652.

12. *Ibid.*, pp. 640–56.

Chapter Three

1. Translated (Lihani) from Carolina Michaëlis de Vasconcellos, *Notas Vicentinas* (Lisbon: Rev. "Ocidente," 1949), p. 470, n. 479.

Notes and References

2. J. H. Parker, *Gil Vicente* (New York: Twayne Publishers, 1967), p. 30, has noted: "It is even possible that Gil Vicente may have witnessed the performance of some of Encina's eclogues in the higher circles of his native land."

3. John Lihani, "Lucas Fernández and the Evolution of the Shepherd's Family Pride in Early Spanish Drama," *Hispanic Review,* XXV (1957), 263.

4. On the one hand the meager data on the life of Lucas Fernández have provided little to clarify this point. Until recently it has been generally believed that Lucas never ventured out of his home town of Salamanca: *no salió de su rincón natal y vivió sin crisis pasionales* (he did not venture from his native nook and lived without emotional crises) according to Guillermo Díaz-Plaja, *Historia general de las literaturas hispánicas,* II (Barcelona: Editorial Barna, 1951), 267. On the other hand, we saw in our Chapter 1 that the presence of Lucas Fernández is documented in Regoim, Portugal, and possibly also in Lisbon.

5. T. R. Hart, in his edition of *Gil Vicente, Obras dramáticas castellanas* (Madrid: Clásicos Castellanos, 1962), p. xiii, suggests that Vicente studied at the University of Salamanca.

6. Aubrey F. G. Bell, *Four Plays of Gil Vicente* (Cambridge University, 1920), p. xl. The quotation reflects the Portuguese spelling used by Bell. For a detailed interpretation of the biographical information contained in the play, see J. Lihani, "Personal Elements in Gil Vicente's *Auto pastoril castellano,*" *Hispanic Review,* XXXVII (1969), 297–303.

7. At the end of the *Auto de la visitación* (*Play of the Visitation*), also known as the *Herdsman's Monologue,* we find the following editorial comment: "And because it was a new thing in Portugal, this play pleased the Queen Mother so much that she asked the author to present it again during the Christmas matins, adapting it to the Birth of the Redeemer. But since the matter was quite different, instead of this, the author wrote the following work [Auto pastoril castellano]." Translated (Lihani) from T. R. Hart, *op. cit.,* p. 6.

8. *quiero aquí poner mi hato,* in T. R. Hart's *Gil Vicente,* p. 7, v. 10. Subsequent quotes from this edition are identified simply with *Vicente.*

9. There has been a difference of opinion on the interpretation of this line. Thomas Hart, *op. cit.,* p. 9, notes that in the *Copilação* of 1562 a marginal note suggests that *Ioã domado dezia por el rey dõ joã segũdo* (*Ioã domado* was said for King John II). Aubrey Bell proposed the reading *dourado* (golden) for *domado* (tamed, subdued), and Paul Teyssier, *La langue de Gil Vicente* (Paris: Klincksieck, 1959), p. 45, interprets it as an error for the sayagués term

adamado (beloved), and adds that it is a pastoral cryptonym for King John II of Portugal. Whereas the word could be interpreted also with the meaning that Teyssier gives it, it seems to us that its first meaning, "tamed, subdued," in particular, and even the other one suggested by Teyssier, are more applicable to Encina than to the King. The reference certainly need not be to John II, the late King, and need not be interpreted as an *ubi sunt* theme in the sense of death (as T. Hart, *op. cit.*, notes, p. 9), but rather as one's simple absence due to having gone to distant lands. We believe the phrase refers to Juan del Encina whose eclipse at the palace of the Duke of Alba and subsequent departure for Rome, via Portugal, does evoke this well-known nostalgic theme, as Gil wonders *¿qué se hizo su corral?* ("Whatever happened to his fold?"). For further details see J. Lihani, "Personal Elements in Gil Vicente's *Auto pastoril castellano*," *Hispanic Review*, XXXVII (1969), 300.

Chapter Four

1. The trope is derived from the Latin *tropus* (turn), which was a combination of four or five Latin verses interpolated into the Mass.

2. The date of the festival varies, and the day is fixed only as the second Thursday after Pentecost—Pentecost being the fiftieth day after Easter.

3. N. D. Shergold, *A History of the Spanish Stage* (Oxford: Oxford University Press, 1967), p. 1.

4. Mary Marguerite Butler, R.S.M., *Hrotsvitha: The Theatricality of Her Plays* (New York: Philosophical Library, 1960), p. 179. In her fine study on the nun Hrotsvitha of Gandersheim, who in the tenth century wrote six comedies modeled on those of Terence, Sister Butler has declared (p. 73): "Research has proved . . . that during [the fourth to the twelfth] centuries, theatre existed in fluctuating emphasis in classical, mimetic, and liturgical forms; that the Church was, in turn, a friend and a foe to the theatre; that Hrotsvitha did not live in a vast dramatic wasteland since within her plays there can be discerned vestiges of the three forms of theatre existing during her day." Comprehensive histories of drama readily confirm the existence of various forms of dramatic productions across the centuries; e.g., N. Díaz de Escobar and Lasso de la Vega, *Historia del teatro español* (Barcelona: Montaner y Simón, 1924), pp. 58–70.

5. "Nor shall the clerics be makers of mockery plays, so that people would come to see how they are done. And if others should put them on, the clerics should not come there, because many villanies and indecencies go on there; nor shall they do likewise in the churches; rather we say they should throw those out in shame who make them, for the Church of God is made for praying and not to

make mockeries within." (Translated [Lihani] from Alfonso X, *Partida I*, título VI, ley 34.)

6. O. B. Hardison, Jr., *Christian Rite and Christian Drama in the Middle Ages* (Baltimore: Johns Hopkins Press, 1965), p. 283.

7. P. Groult and V. Emond, *La Littérature française du moyen âge* (Gembloux: J. Duculot, 1948), p. 209.

8. R. B. Donovan, *The Liturgical Drama in Medieval Spain* (Toronto: Pontifical Institute of Mediaeval Studies, 1958).

9. W. Leonard Grant, *Neo-Latin Literature and the Pastoral* (Chapel Hill: University of North Carolina Press, 1965).

10. Hardison, p. 292.

11. We find the word *juego* used repeatedly and rather freely in the accounts of the Church Council. It was applied loosely to any sort of public entertainment, whether a dance, dramatic piece, song, or still life representations on floats, etc. Sometimes, instead of *juego*, a synonymous term was *invención*, and another, though rarely used, was the term *auto*. It was employed with the same connotations that today we find in the word "act" when we speak of a performer's "act." In the terminology of the time, *auto* was not restricted to a dramatic piece, but could be used to designate other performances as well, including the dance. Thus, *juego, invención,* and *auto* were used to denote almost any type of amusement; act, diversion, entertainment, performance, spectacle, contest, etc.

12. Espinosa, p. 574.

13. *Ibid.,* p. 406; *En qué consistieron estos juegos no dudamos en afirmar: [. . .] En la* "Comedia *fecha por Lucas Fernández.*"

14. Money was paid to Lucas Fernández, "cantor, for the play of the shepherds that he made [for] this festivity" (*a lucas fernandez, Cantor del abto de los pastores que fiso la dicha fiesta*), Espinosa, p. 577.

15. Shergold, p. 85. R. Espinosa Maeso suggested that it might very well have been the *Farsa del Soldado* (*The Farce of the Soldier*) which he conjectures was written about that time. According to our best information, however, it was written about six years earlier, but as the first *Comedia*, it was most assuredly presented several times and could have been the one alluded to on this occasion (Espinosa, p. 408).

16. The *arca* was an important center of attraction. There is an item that tells of eight men carrying torches before it in the procession. It was the coffer or chest that symbolically represented Christ's sepulchre and served to hold the "body of Christ," the consecrated Host for the Eucharist. We find the term *arca* used for Christ's tomb in an Easter play by Juan del Encina: ". . . this is His sepulchre/ treasure of our life . . . O divine sacrarium/ chest of very great

treasure/ neither of silver nor of gold/ but of a much higher metal."
(Translated [Lihani] from the *Cancionero* of 1496, facsimile edition
with prologue by E. Cotarelo y Mori (Madrid: Real Academia
Española, 1928, fol. 106 vº).

17. The use of arrows is explained by the biography of the saint. He
had been an officer in the Praetorian Guard, and subsequently became
an ardent Christian. In 288 A.D. Diocletian ordered him to be put to
death. Though pierced with arrows, he struggled for recovery and
then was clubbed to death.

18. *Momos* derived from the Latin *momus* which was originally a
gesture, grimace, or jeer, usually made in plays, dances, or masquer-
ades for amusement. In the first half of the fifteenth century in Spain,
the word came to designate, as is here seen, the programs and amusements that then became popular. *Momos* (mummers) then signified
groups of people usually wearing masks and dressed in colorful, even
psychedelic costumes, as of fine white linen engraved with flames of
fire, or of short black mantles embroidered with figured representations.

19. I. S. Révah, "Manifestations théâtrales pré-vicentine: Les
'Momos' de 1500," *Bulletin d'Histoire du Théâtre Portugais,* III
(1952), 91–105.

20. Espinosa Maeso suggests that this short play might have been
the *Representación del amor* composed by Juan del Encina, which
was written to be played before Prince John, son of the Catholic Kings,
and which is believed to have been the play that Encina presented
also in Rome in Cardinal Arborea's house, and not the *Plácida y
Vitoriano* eclogue which has been generally believed to be the play
given on that occasion (Espinosa, p. 403).

21. Espinosa, p. 580.

22. *Fuera del tablado, y en el coro, hallábase el árbol del Paraíso
con las figuras de Adán y Eva, y encima de dicho árbol aparecía
también el Niño Jesús, rodeado de serafines* (Offstage, and in the
choir, there was the tree of Paradise with the figures of Adam and
Eve, and above the said tree there appeared also the Child Jesus,
surrounded by seraphims.) Quoted from W. H. Shoemaker, *The
Multiple Stage in Spain During the Fifteenth and Sixteenth Centuries* (Princeton: Princeton University Press, 1935), p. 31.

23. Espinosa, p. 582.

24. *Ibid.*

25. *Ibid.*, p. 585.

26. *rrepresentó el bobo en vn auto día de corpus christi* ("he
played the fool in a performance on Corpus Christi Day"), (Espinosa,
p. 405).

Chapter Five

1. H. López Morales, *Tradición y creación en los orígenes del teatro castellano* (Madrid: Ediciones Alcalá, 1968), p. 119.

2. W. H. Shoemaker discusses all sorts of settings in *The Multiple Stage in Spain during the Fifteenth and Sixteenth Centuries* (Princeton: Princeton University Press, 1935).

3. William C. Bryant, "Lucas Fernández and the Early Spanish Drama," University of California (Berkeley), Ph.D. dissertation, 1964, (Ann Arbor, Mich.: University Microfilms, Inc., 1965); *Dissertation Abstracts*, XXV, no. 11 (Ann Arbor, Mich.: University Microfilms, Inc., 1965), 6616.

4. G. Cirot, "Le Théâtre Religieux d'Encina," *Bulletin Hispanique*, XLIII (1941), 11.

5. The following studies vary in depth and extent on the topic of the *sayagués* dialect:

Dámaso Alonso, ed., Gil Vicente, *Tragicomedia de Don Duardos* (Madrid: Consejo Superior de Investigaciones Científicas, 1941), pp. 117–54.

J. E. Gillet, *Propalladia and Other Works of Bartolomé de Torres Naharro*, 4 vols. (Bryn Mawr and Philadelphia: University of Pennsylvania Press, 1943–1961). This thorough work contains a tremendous amount of excellent information scattered throughout the volumes.

José Lamano y Beneite, *El dialecto vulgar salmantino* (Salamanca: Tipografía Popular, 1915).

John Lihani, "Glossary of the *Farsas y églogas* of Lucas Fernández," University of Texas, unpublished doctoral dissertation, 1954.

————,*El lenguaje de Lucas Fernández; estudio del dialecto sayagués* (Bogotá: Instituto Caro y Cuervo, in press).

————, "Some Notes on *Sayagués*," *Hispania*, XLI (1958), 165–69.

O. T. Myers, "Senor in Sayagués," *Modern Language Notes*, LXXX (1965), 271–73.

M. Romera-Navarro, "*Quillotro* y sus variantes," *Hispanic Review*, II (1934), 217–25.

Charlotte Stern, "Studies on the Sayagués in the Early Spanish Drama," University of Pennsylvania, microfilmed doctoral dissertation, 1960.

————, "Sayago and *Sayagués* in Spanish History and Literature," *Hispanic Review*, XXIX (1961), 217–37.

Paul Teyssier, *La langue de Gil Vicente* (Paris: Klincksieck, 1959).

Frida Weber de Kurlat, "El dialecto sayagués y los críticos," *Filología*, I (1949), 43–50.

————, "Latinismos arrusticados en el sayagués," *Nueva Revista de Filología Hispánica*, I (1947), 166–70.

6. F. Weber de Kurlat, *Lo cómico en el teatro de Fernán González de Eslava* (Buenos Aires: University of Buenos Aires, 1963), p. 65.

7. This is a bona fide dialectal form; see O. T. Myers, "Senor in *Sayagués,*" *Modern Language Notes,* LXX (1965), 271–73.

8. John Lihani, "The Question of Authorship of the *Coplas* Attributed to Lucas Fernández," *Kentucky Foreign Language Quarterly,* XII (1965), 238–45.

9. O. T. Myers, "Juan del Encina and the *Auto del repelón,*" *Hispanic Review,* XXXII (1964), 189–201.

10. Translated (Lihani) from Lamano y Beneite, *op. cit.,* p. 13.

11. R. Menéndez Pidal, "Estudio del dialecto leonés," *Revista de Archivos, Bibliotecas y Museos,* XIV (1906), 142.

12. J. Lihani, "Some Notes on *Sayagués,*" *Hispania,* XLI (1958), 165–69.

Chapter Six

1. There are parallelisms on the definition of love with earlier works, such as Juan Ruiz' *Libro de buen amor* (strophes 398–405), and with Encina's poem "Nuevas te trayo, carillo," found in the *Egloga pastoril valenciana,* edited by E. Kohler in *Sieben spanische dramatische Eklogen* (Dresden: M. Niemeyer, 1911), p. 287. A similar attitude toward the tribulations of love is found after Fernández' work in the anonymous sentimental novel, *Questión de amor* (1513), published in the *Nueva Biblioteca de Autores Españoles,* VII (Madrid: Bailly-Baillière, 1907), pp. 67–73; and then there is a recognizable parallel of social protest between the *Farce of Prabos and the Soldier* and a later creation by Bartolomé de Torres Naharro, the *Comedia Soldadesca.* In the farce by Lucas we note the following rebuke to the Soldado: "And you dare to steal,/ and rob,/ and eat by others' sweat of brow" (Translated [Lihani] from *Farsas,* p. 108, vv. 444–46), while in the *Comedia Soldadesca* of Torres Naharro, written some dozen years later, we find an expression in the same vein: "You, lords,/ live amidst many sufferings,/ and you are more wealthy of pains,/ and you eat from the sweat/ of others' poor hands" (Translated [Lihani] from *Propalladia,* II, 143.

2. A similar technique had been used earlier by Fernando de Rojas, *La Celestina,* ed. J. Cejador y Frauca (Madrid: Clásicos Castellanos, 1941), II, 211, where Pleberio winds up his complaint against Love by naming characters who suffered at its hands and then cuts himself short, *Otros muchos, que callo, porque tengo harto que contar en mi mal* ("Many others whom I omit, because I have enough to tell about my own misfortune"). Lucas Fernández' familiarity with *La Celestina* is evident on other occasions as well. This fact would tend

to date his play at around 1499, unless Lucas was aware of the work by Rojas before its first publication in that year.

3. The medicines listed are: *madresilva, gamones, rábano, encienso, macho, bayones, flor de sago, doradilla, manzanilla* (honeysuckle, asphodel, radish, incense, male-plant, reed mace, flower of salvia, ceterach, chamomile). Some of these as the *manzanilla* are tealike medicines to strengthen the stomach. The properties of the others and their values have been lost to us and remain in the obscure chapters of medieval and Renaissance medical books.

Whether their function was misunderstood and misapplied by the shepherd (to the delight of the audience) is difficult to tell, yet we may assume that they were not to be taken in earnest, but rather for their humorous connotations inasmuch as they were used to cure the illness of Pascual's she-ass.

4. Alfonso X, *Las Siete Partidas,* trans. Samuel Parsons Scott (New York: Commerce Clearing House, Inc., 1931), pp. 887–88: "Consent alone, with the desire to marry, constitutes matrimony between a man and a woman. . . . Matrimony can be contracted by the parties themselves . . . and it should be done openly and not secretly so that it can be proved" (*Partida* IV, Title II, Law V).

5. Fernando del Pulgar, *Crónica de los Reyes Católicos,* II, ed. Juan de Mata Carriazo (Madrid: Espasa Calpe, 1943), 74.

6. Hermenegildo, "Nueva interpretación de un primitivo Lucas Fernández," *Segismundo,* no. 3, pp. 1–34; López Morales, *Tradición y creación en los orígenes del teatro castellano* (Madrid: Ediciones Alcalá, 1968), pp. 190–97.

7. See Cotarelo, p. xxii of his edition of the *Farsas y églogas.*

8. *Propalladia,* ed. J. E. Gillet, IV, 473.

9. *Ibid.,* I, 83.

Chapter Seven

1. J. E. Gillet, *Propalladia,* IV, 38, 355, places the tentative limiting dates for the work between 1498 and 1500.

2. H. López Morales, *Tradición y creación en los orígenes del teatro castellano* (Madrid: Ediciones Alcalá, 1968), pp. 167–70.

3. That presenting plays at weddings was a well-established practice is confirmed by an artistically excellent and thematically beautiful play of Lope de Vega, an outstanding masterpiece of the theater, *El castigo sin venganza* (1631), in which Lope depicts the tragic events that transpired in Ferrara, Italy, in May of 1425, when Gómez Manrique, one of the early dramatists, was just a child and had yet to blaze a trail in Spanish drama. What interests us at the moment in this dramatic piece by Lope is the fact that the Duke

of Ferrara includes a play in his plans for entertainment at his own wedding. As the Duke dictates that the play shall be one of the several entertainments at his nuptials, he laughingly enjoins that there be none of the usual vulgarity seen in other plays. This immediately recalls the bawdy *introitos* of Torres Naharro's plays, and some scenes from Lucas' performances containing vulgarity presumably because the audience liked it. Bartolomé de Torres Naharro's plays are known to be full of what until recently were considered abominable obscenities. Today's modern audiences, as those of Torres Naharro, apparently took those in stride. Such displays of a sensual or lewd nature were almost a ritualistic practice at weddings in Italy, and this is what fostered the Duke's remarks.

In the first act of Lope's play, we see presented on the stage a company of Italian actors who rehearse scenes before the Duke of Ferrara. The latter tires of this and sternly dismisses them. If we are to put faith in Lope's further remarks in the play (and sometimes he advises us that he takes the trouble to depict the events as he has researched them), we shall believe that actors in the first third of the fifteenth century were highly esteemed in Italy and apparently well paid. In Act II of the play, a confidante remarks to the Duchess of Ferrara that her husband orders the "most costly" entertainment for her, and specifically refers to the actors who are then staying in the household for the purpose of presenting their play for her and her company. All the action of Act II, in fact, takes place on a balcony just outside the palace room overlooking a courtyard where the play is being performed. See Lope Félix de Vega Carpio, *Obras escogidas,* ed. F. C. Sainz de Robles (Madrid: M. Aguilar, 1946). pp. 913–48.

4. Luis Ortiz Behety, "El teatro de Lucas Fernández," *Boletín de Estudios de Teatro,* nos. 24–25 (1949), p. 37.

5. A. Valbuena Prat, *Historia de la literature española,* 6th ed. (Barcelona: Gustavo Gili, 1960), I, 368.

6. Prince John, who died in October of 1497, was born on June 20, 1478, according to Fernando del Pulgar, *Crónica de los Reyes Católicos,* I, edited by Juan de Mata Carriazo (Madrid: Espasa Calpe, 1943), 325. Other chroniclers place his death in early November. Cf. Alonso de Santa Cruz, *Crónica de los Reyes Católicos,* I, ed. Juan de Mata Carriazo (Sevilla, 1951), 167.

7. Translated [Lihani] from Alicio Garcítoral, *La España de los Reyes Católicos* (Buenos Aires: Editorial Claridad, 1950), p. 158.

8. Eugen Kohler, ed., *Representaciones de Juan del Encina* (Strasbourg: Heitz & Mündel, 1913), p. 9.

9. The original music and words of the *villancico* retained here in the refrain may be the work of Garcí-Sánchez de Badajoz (1406?–

1526?). See Francisco Asenjo Barbieri, *Cancionero musical español de los siglos XV y XVI* (Madrid: Tip. de los Huérfanos, 1890), no. 360. The use of Barbieri's name hereafter refers to his *Cancionero*.

10. William H. Prescott tells us about Prince Juan in the twentieth year of his life when he married Princess Margaret of Austria. He and his father, Fernando, had ridden with their entourage on horseback to the northern frontier of Spain where the two awaited and finally welcomed the Princess in Santander in the month of March of 1497. They traveled overland back to Castile where the carefully planned wedding took place on April 3, 1497. The nuptials were celebrated with great feasts, tourneys, tilts, and many other spectacles. Several months later, the Prince of Asturias (as the heir to the throne was titled) arrived in Salamanca with his young bride. There were widespread public festivities in the city to welcome him, but in the midst of this public display of affection he was seized with a fever. Speedily the symptoms assumed an alarming character. When his father arrived in Salamanca, there were no hopes entertained for the Prince's recovery. "Ferdinand, however, endeavored to cheer his son with hope which he did not feel himself; but the young prince told him that it was too late to be deceived; that he was prepared to part with a world which, in its best estate, was filled with vanity and vexation; and that all he now desired was that his parents might feel the same sincere resignation to the divine will which he experienced himself." W. H. Prescott, *History of the Reign of Ferdinand and Isabella, the Catholic* (Philadelphia: J. B. Lippincott Co., 1878), p. 357.

11. The music for the two *villancicos* of the *Égloga VIII* composed by Juan del Encina can be appreciated in Barbieri, nos. 353 and 354.

12. Charlotte Stern, "Some New Thoughts on the Early Spanish Drama," *Bulletin of the Comediantes*, XVII (Spring 1966), 16.

Chapter Eight

1. This can be seen in many studies including one by Sandro Sticca, "The *Planctus Mariae* and the Passion Play," *Symposium*, XV (Spring 1961), 41–47.

2. Two of the recent editions are (1) *Auto de la Pasión* published by the Vice-Secretariat of Public Education (Madrid: Aguirre, 1942); (2) José Fradejas Lebrero, ed., *Teatro religioso medieval* (Tetuán: Editorial Cremades, 1956).

3. This is the interpretation of Alfredo Hermenegildo, "Nueva interpretación de un primitivo Lucas Fernández," *Segismundo*, no. 3, p. 18.

4. Comments on stage settings can be found in N. D. Shergold,

A History of the Spanish Stage (Oxford: Oxford University Press, 1967), pp. 7–8, 12–16, 18–20, 60–67.

5. R. B. Williams, in *The Staging of Plays in the Spanish Peninsula Prior to 1555* (Iowa City: Iowa University Press, 1935), tells of the scene of the plays, but it is difficult to describe the possible varied staging of each. W. H. Shoemaker, in his work, *The Multiple Stage in Spain during the Fifteenth and Sixteenth Centuries* (Princeton, 1935), shows that the staging, even on multiple, simultaneous stages, was in use and could at times be quite elaborate.

6. In Spain both Iñigo de Mendoza and Juan del Encina had dealt to varying degrees with the Passion. Encina composed his *Égloga III* entitled *Representación a la muy bendita passión y muerte de nuestro precioso Redentor* (*Representation to the Very Blessed Passion and Death of Our Precious Redeemer*). See H. López Morales, ed., *Églogas de Juan del Enzina* (Madrid: Escelicer, 1963), p. 45. Encina's play is almost prosaic, and in no way can compare with the emotion, fullness of sentiment, and lyricism shown in Fernández' play.

7. Sandro Sticca, "The *Planctus Mariae* and the Passion Play," *Symposium*, XV (1961), 41–47.

8. Manuel Cañete, *Teatro español del siglo XVI* (Madrid: Imp. de M. Tello, 1885), p. 86.

9. A. Hermenegildo, "Nueva interpretación de un primitivo Lucas Fernández," *Segismundo*, no. 3, pp. 1–34.

10. A. Valbuena Prat notes that "In the course of the work, Fernández has combined, allegorically, persons from the *Old Testament* —Jeremiah—with those of the New, anticipating the procedure of the sacramental plays, it being of interest that one of Calderón's works— *A Dios por razón de estado*—coincides with the detail of St. Dionysius Areopagita attesting to the divinity of the Redeemer." Translated [Lihani] from *Historia de la literatura española*, 6th ed. (Barcelona: Gustavo Gili, 1960), I, 372.

Chapter Nine

1. W. L. Grant, "Neo-Latin Biblical Pastorals," *Studies in Philology*, LVIII (1961), 25–43.

2. Manuel Cañete, *Teatro español del siglo XVI* (Madrid: Imp. de M. Tello, 1885), p. 69.

3. For a discussion of this type of character, see Michael J. Ruggerio, *The Evolution of the Go-Between in Spanish Literature through the Sixteenth Century* (Berkeley: University of California Press, 1966).

4. Translated [Lihani] from González Pedroso, "Autos sacramentales

desde su origen hasta fines del siglo XVII," p. xi, as cited by Cañete, p. lxxxiii.

5. Frida Weber de Kurlat, *Lo cómico en el teatro de Fernán González de Eslava* (Buenos Aires: University of Buenos Aires, 1963), pp. 149–64.

6. *Farsas*, p. 133.

7. E. Cotarelo y Mori, ed., *Lucas Fernández, "Farsas y églogas," Prólogo*, p. xx.

8. Translated [Lihani] from *Farsas*, p. 128, vv. 291–95.

9. Charlotte Stern, "Iñigo de Mendoza and Medieval Dramatic Ritual," *Hispanic Review*, XXXIII (1965), 228, n. 70.

10. *Ibid.*

11. *Ibid.*, p. 228.

Chapter Ten

1. Antonio de Nebrija, *Gramática castellana*, ed., Pascual Galindo Romero and Luis Ortiz Muñoz (Madrid: Edición de la Junta del Centenario, 1946), p. 57.

2. Juan del Encina, *Cancionero*, facsimile of 1496 edition with prologue by E. Cotarelo y Mori (Madrid: Real Academia Española, 1928), fol., aii rº.

3. We use this designation for *Églogas de Juan del Enzina*, ed., Humberto López-Morales (Madrid: Escelicer, 1963).

4. Angel Valbuena Prat, *Historia del teatro español* (Barcelona: Noguer, 1956), p. 24.

5. *Nueva Biblioteca de Autores Españoles*, VII (Madrid: Bailly-Baillière, 1907), 41–98, but in particular 67–73.

6. Fernando de Rojas, *La Celestina*, ed., Julio Cejador y Frauca (Madrid: Clásicos Castellanos, 1931), II, 59.

7. Juan Ruiz, Arcipreste de Hita, *Libro de buen amor*, ed., Julio Cejador y Frauca (Madrid: Clásicos Castellanos, 1946), II, 75.

8. Gil Vicente, *Obras dramáticas castellanas*, ed., Thomas R. Hart (Madrid: Clásicos Castellanos, 1962), p. 14.

9. This is discussed in J. Lihani, "Personal Elements in Gil Vicente's *Auto pastoril castellano*," *Hispanic Review*, XXXVII (1969), 297–303.

10. Iñigo de Mendoza, "Vita Christi," in *Nueva Biblioteca de Autores Españoles*, XIX (Madrid: Bailly-Baillière, 1912), 22.

11. N. D. Shergold, *A History of the Spanish Stage* (Oxford: Oxford University Press, 1967), p. 145.

12. Joseph E. Gillet, *Propalladia and Other Works of Bartolomé de Torres Naharro*, completed by Otis H. Green, IV (Philadelphia: University of Pennsylvania Press, 1961), 471.

13. Laurence Keates, *The Court Theatre of Gil Vicente* (Lisbon: Author, 1962), p. 86.
14. *Ibid.*, p. 87.

Chapter Eleven

1. Maxim Newmark, *Dictionary of Spanish Literature* (New York: Philosophical Library, 1956), p. 150.

Selected Bibliography

PRIMARY SOURCES

1. Editions of Fernández' Works

CAÑETE, MANUEL, ed. *Lucas Fernández, Farsas y églogas* (Madrid: Imprenta Nacional, 1867). The only edition of Fernández' plays that was available for an entire century. It contains an introduction on the early theater and a glossary of dialectal terms appearing in the book.

COTARELO Y MORI, EMILIO, ed. *Lucas Fernández, "Farsas y églogas"* (Madrid: Real Academia Española, 1929). A facsimile edition of the 1514 Salamancan princeps with a brief but useful introduction. Valuable edition for its faithful reproduction of the unique copy now in existence of the original edition.

DÍAZ-PLAJA, GUILLERMO. *Antología mayor de la literatura española*, I, "Edad Media" (siglos X-XV), (Madrid: Editorial Labor, 1958). Contains each one of the plays by Lucas Fernández, but all of them are printed with several omissions.

FERNÁNDEZ, LUCAS. *Farsas y églogas, al modo y estilo pastoril y castellano* (Salamanca: Lorenço de Liomdedei, 1514). Invaluable unique copy of the princeps edition maintained in the rare book room of the National Library in Madrid.

————. *Auto de la Pasión* (Madrid: Vicesecretaría de educación popular, 1942). Modern version of the sacramental play with a brief introduction on the playwright.

FRADEJAS LEBRERO, JOSÉ. *Teatro religioso medieval* (Tetuán: Editorial Cremades, 1956). Included among the three edited plays is Fernández' *Passion Play*. (See immediately preceding entry.)

GALLARDO, BARTOLOMÉ J. *El Criticón*, nos. 4, 5, 7 (Madrid: Author, 1859–1867). Contains some complete plays as well as portions of others by Lucas Fernández.

LIHANI, JOHN, ed. *Lucas Fernández, "Farsas y églogas"* (New York: Las Américas Publishing Co., 1969). The only complete critical edition of Lucas Fernández' plays with an introduction and notes.

SECONDARY SOURCES

1. Books and Articles about Fernández

BEHETY, LUIS ORTIZ. "El teatro de Lucas Fernández," *Boletín de Estudios de Teatro*, nos. 24–25 (1949), pp. 37–39. A very brief appraisal of Lucas Fernández' theater and his *Passion Play* in particular.

BRYANT, WILLIAM C. *Lucas Fernández and the Early Spanish Drama* (Ann Arbor, Mich.: University Microfilm, Inc., 1965). A Ph.D. dissertation, University of California, 1964. Good critical introduction to the dramatist with a transcription of his plays.

Chancelaria de D. Manuel I, manuscript (1513–1516), archives of Torre do Tombo, Lisbon, Portugal. Contains a letter of privileges granted to Lucas Fernández, "inhabitant of Regoim." It may very well involve the author of the *Farsas y églogas*.

CIROT, G. "L'*Auto de la pasión* de Lucas Fernández," *Bulletin Hispanique*, XLII (1940), 285–91. Recounts the plot and appraises the work of exceptional literary merit.

ENCINA, JUAN DEL. *Cancionero*, facsimile of 1496 edition with a prologue by E. Cotarelo y Mori (Madrid: Real Academia Española, 1928). Cotarelo y Mori mentions some data from Lucas Fernández' life as they touch upon that of Encina.

ESPINOSA MAESO, RICARDO. "Ensayo biográfico del Maestro Lucas Fernández," *Boletín de la Real Academia Española*, X (1923), 386–424 and 567–603. The only well-documented study of the dramatist's life.

——. "Nuevos datos biográficos de Juan del Encina," *Boletín de la Real Academia Española*, VIII (1921), 640–56. Includes likewise pertinent data on the life of Lucas Fernández.

FERNÁNDEZ, ANTONIA. "Acerca de la fecha de composición de la *Farsa o cuasi comedia del Soldado* de Lucas Fernández," *Filología*, XI (1968), 121–218. On the basis of socio-historical allusions, the author attempts, inconclusively, to place the date of composition of this play between 1507 and 1508.

HERMENEGILDO, ALFREDO. "Nueva interpretación de un primitivo, Lucas Fernández," *Segismundo*, no. 3, pp. 1–34. An outstanding interpretive, critical study of the *Auto de la pasión* in particular.

LIHANI, JOHN. "Lucas Fernández and the Evolution of the Shepherd's Family Pride in Early Spanish Drama," *Hispanic Review*, XXV (1957), 252–63. Pinpoints Fernández' literary relationship with Gil Vicente and other early playwrights.

Selected Bibliography

————. "Personal Elements in Gil Vicente's *Auto pastoril castellano*," *Hispanic Review*, XXXVII (1969), 297–303. Textual interpretation is used to suggest the presence of Lucas Fernández in the Portuguese court.

LÓPEZ MORALES, HUMBERTO. *Tradición y creación en los orígenes del teatro castellano* (Madrid: Ediciones Alcalá, 1968). Discusses favorably many aspects of the theater of Lucas Fernández in relation to its broad development in Spain.

MICHAËLIS DE VASCONCELLOS, CAROLINA. *Notas Vicentinas* (Lisbon: Rev. "Ocidente," 1949). An extensive work that deals with much more than its modest title indicates; includes important items on Lucas Fernández' life and work.

STERN, CHARLOTTE. "Iñigo de Mendoza and Medieval Dramatic Ritual," *Hispanic Review*, XXXIII (1965), 197–245. Contains items from Lucas Fernández' drama relative to the development of the Spanish medieval theater.

WEBER DE KURLAT, FRIDA. *Lo cómico en el teatro de Fernán González de Eslava* (Buenos Aires: University of Buenos Aires, 1963). Contains many references to the contributions made by Lucas Fernández to the early Spanish theater.

2. Background Material

CAÑETE, MANUEL. *Teatro español del siglo XVI* (Madrid: Imprenta de M. Tello, 1885). One of the earliest and still useful attempts at the history of the sixteenth-century Spanish theater.

CRAWFORD, J. P. W. *Spanish Drama before Lope de Vega* (Philadelphia: University of Pennsylvania Press, 1937). An indispensable reference text for the early theater in the vernacular. It was re-issued in 1967 with a bibliographical supplement by Warren T. McCready.

DONOVAN, R. B. *The Liturgical Drama in Medieval Spain* (Toronto: Pontifical Institute of Mediaeval Studies, 1958). Traces the liturgical theater to the tropes of the Mass.

GILLET, JOSEPH E. *Propalladia and Other Works of Bartolomé de Torres Naharro*, 4 vols. Last volume completed by Otis H. Green. (Bryn Mawr and Philadelphia: University of Pennsylvania Press, 1943–1961). Large amount of varied valuable information and penetrating criticism on the Spanish drama is contained throughout the volumes.

SHERGOLD, N. D. *A History of the Spanish Stage* (Oxford: Oxford University Press, 1967). Extensive and authoritative critical study of the Spanish drama from the Middle Ages through the Golden Age.

SHOEMAKER, W. H. *The Multiple Stage in Spain during the Fifteenth and Sixteenth Centuries* (Princeton: Princeton University Press, 1935). A carefully elaborated account of the evidence available on the staging of the plays.

VALBUENA PRAT, ANGEL. *Historia del teatro español* (Barcelona: Noguer, 1956). Good compilation of the contributions of many playwrights. Fine critical viewpoint.

WARDROPPER, BRUCE W. *Introducción al teatro religioso del Siglo de Oro* (Madrid: Revista de Occidente, 1953). A lucid discussion of the development of the Spanish religious theater.

WILLIAMS, RONALD B. *The Staging of Plays in the Spanish Peninsula Prior to 1555* (Iowa City: University of Iowa Press, 1935). Clarifies types of performances of the early plays. A valuable work.

3. Language Studies

LAMANO Y BENEITE, JOSÉ DE. *El dialecto vulgar salmantino* (Salamanca: Tipografía Popular, 1915). An early attempt at a study of the Salamancan *charro* dialect with a list of dialectal terms. Inadequate in its linguistic analysis.

LIHANI, JOHN. *El lenguaje de Lucas Fernández; estudio del dialecto sayagués* (Bogotá: Instituto Caro y Cuervo, in press). Thorough linguistic study of the dramatist's language, together with a glossary containing numerous examples illustrating word usage across the centuries.

MENÉNDEZ PIDAL, RAMÓN. "Estudio del dialecto leonés," *Revista de Archivos, Bibliotecas y Museos,* X (1906), 294–311. Initial effort at a description of the Leonese dialect.

STERN, CHARLOTTE. *Studies in the Sayagués in the Early Spanish Drama* (Ann Arbor, Mich.: University Microfilms, Inc., 1960). A Ph.D. dissertation, University of Pennsylvania, 1960. Fine contribution to the study of the *sayagués.*

TEYSSIER, PAUL. *La langue de Gil Vicente* (Paris: Klinksieck, 1959). Careful study of the Portuguese dramatist's language with many examples from the work of Lucas Fernández.

Index

Index

dogma, 125, 127–28, 149
Domado, Juan, 46
Donovan, R. B., 53
Doñinos, 73
dowries, 90, 92, 133–34, 139
drama, Classical Latin, 51–53, 146;
  European medieval, 51; Greek,
  51; Italian 140, 141; Latin, 51,
  146; liturgical, 52, 149; popular,
  50, 147; secular, 52, 54, 89;
  vernacular, 51–53
Duardos, Don, 142

Easter, 64, 106; play, 54, 110–11,
  113–14
Ecce homo, 107, 109, 111
echarse pullas, 91
eclogue, 121, 141
Eclogue of the Nativity (Egloga del
  nacimiento), 65, 67, 73, 119, 125–
  26, 129
Egloga I, 36; VIII, 105; XIV, 140
Egloga de Febea, 80
Egloga de Fileno y Céfira, 79
Egloga de las grandes lluvias, 36–37
Egloga representada en requesta de
  unos amores, 79
Encina, Francisco de, 22
Encina, Juan del, 21–22, 29, 34–39,
  41–42, 44–46, 49, 51–52, 57, 63,
  72, 74, 76–77, 79–80, 88, 96, 100–
  101, 103, 105, 110, 121, 131–42,
  145–46, 148, 150
England, 70, 151
entertainers, 148
entremés, 83
Epiphany, 128
Epístolas familiares, 143
Espinosa Maeso, Ricardo, 17–18,
  20, 25, 32, 34, 39, 50, 55, 63–64,
  91
Eucharist, 149–50
Evangelists, 60, 110
Eve, 61, 136
exempla, 125

Fables, 143
Faith, 100, 111–12, 114, 123, 150
' farce (farsa), 52, 94, 121, 124, 140

Farce of Prabos and the Soldier
  (Farsa del Soldado), 65, 67, 83,
  92, 97, 133, 144
Farce of the Gentleman (Farsa del
  Caballero) see The Maiden's Farce
Farces and eclogues (Farsas y églo-
  gas), 43, 65, 76
Farsa del sacramento, 58
Febea, 80
Ferdinand of Aragón, 34, 41
Fermoselle, Diego de, 21, 29, 35,
  38
France, 70
Francisco de Salamanca, 37
free will, 149
Fuenterrabía, Battle of, 29

García Lorca, F., 111
Ghent, 130
gift, rustic, 128; wedding, 133–34
Gillet, Joseph E., 88, 142
Ginés, San, 124
Goes, Damião de, 41
Golden Age, 63, 72, 74, 76, 92, 110,
  138, 141, 143–44, 146
Gontinos, 73
González, Alonso (Lucas Fernández'
  father), 18–19
González, Salvador, 24
González Pedroso, E., 123
gracioso, 63, 129–30, 143–44
Grant, W. L., 53, 118
Greece, 103; Greek, 125
Guevara, Antonio de, 129, 142–43,
  150
Guinean, 61

hagiographic material, 124
Hardison, Jr., O. B., 52–53
Heaven, 60–61
Hell, 60–61
Hercules, 119
Herdsman's Monologue, The, 43, 51
Hermenegildo, Alfredo, 84, 111–13
hermit, 120, 125, 127
Herod, 144
Hilario, San, 124
Holy Communion, 108
Holy Land, 81

Rueda, Lope de, 63, 77, 94, 121, 132
Ruiz, Juan, 110, 121, 132–33, 137, 139, 143
rustics, 99; accomplishments of, 95; theatrical, 60

Salamanca, 18–20, 23–25, 27–28, 35, 37–39, 42–43, 54–56, 60, 62, 65, 72–74, 76, 101, 109, 121–22, 124, 131, 140, 147–48; Cathedral of, 17, 19, 21, 23, 33, 36–37, 46–47, 55–56, 64, 109, 122; University of, 17, 21, 28–30, 49, 64, 147–48
Sacred Host, 71, 108
Samson, 119
Sánchez, Cristóbal, 55, 59; Diego, 58; Lorénzo, 26; María, 18
Santillana, Marqués de, 131
satire of clergy, 97, 150
Sayago, 74
sayagués, 74, 77, 140, 150
scenes, divisions into, 149
Sebastián, San, 54–57, 59–60
serranas, 57; serrano, 97
serranillas, 133
shepherd, 62–63, 72, 75–76, 89, 93–99, 101–2, 104, 109, 118, 120–21, 123, 127–29, 136, 138–39, 143–45; characteristics of, 95, 121–26, 143
Shergold, N. D., 140
Siete Partidas, 52, 63, 81
slapstick, 87, 149
soldier (soldado), 72, 83–84, 87, 144, 150; boastful, see miles gloriosus; Swiss, 59, 82
song drama, 135, 148
songs, 67, 69, 73, 81, 92, 96, 104–5, 111, 124, 126, 128, 130, 133–34, 149
stage, 109–10; devices, 147; directions, 69, 71, 130, 150; setting, 110
Stern, Charlotte, 130
Sticca, Sandro, 110
suicide, 95
synalepha, 75

Talavera, Archpriest of, see Martínez de Toledo, Alfonso
Tejares, 60
Terence, 51
threats, 86–87
Toledo, 29, 41
Tomás Cantuariense, Santo, 25–28
tordión 55; estordión, 57, 59; turdión, 62; Tordión, Cristóbal, 55
Tormes, River, 27
Toro, Pedro de, 57
Torre do Tombo, 28
Torres Naharro, Bartolomé de, 25, 49, 74, 88, 94, 137, 139, 141–42, 145, 150
Torrijos, Fernando de, 21, 36
tragedy, 69
tragicomedia, 141
triunfo del amor, El, 79
Trojan, 80
troubadours, 67
tropes, 50–54
Turks, 81

unities, Classical, 71, 149
Urban IV, Pope, 50
Urdemalas, Pedro de, 125

Valbuena Prat, A., 100, 135
Val de Villoría, 73
Valencia, 17, 61
Valladolid, 31
Vega, Lope de, 77, 111, 143
verb, conditional, 75; future, 75; use of, 115, 150
vernacular, 50, 52
versification, 65–68
Vicente, Gil, 27, 34, 38, 40, 42–49; 51, 57, 97, 112, 119, 129–30, 137–39, 145, 148, 150; as Gil Terrón, 45, 48
Vico-Nuño, 73
Villa de Alcácer, 42
villancico, 67–68, 81, 91, 93, 99–100, 104, 107, 120, 128, 130, 133–35
Villano del Danubio, 129
Virgin Mary, 78, 106–7, 113, 120, 125, 128

Index